Praise for

A Manager's Guide to

―――――――――――――――◼―――――――――――――――

"This book does a great job of examining an area of leadership often overlooked by new (and seasoned) managers. Practical, and easy to read, it lays out a management concept that can positively impact employees and ultimately the bottom line."

—Stephanie Heffernan, Executive Producer,
E-Commerce, Discovery Communications, Inc.

"Practical. Insightful. Entertaining. This no-nonsense look at coaching is a must read. Not only for those who manage others, but for anyone that hopes to help the people they work with to be more."

—Carole Dickert-Scherr, Vice President,
Human Resources, PBS (Public Broadcast Service)

"Brian Emerson and Anne Loehr are the leaders you need for coaching your team to victory. Their thorough but easy to understand guide sets out the steps you need to take to make sure you have motivated and successful employees. The key is realizing that coaching in not about telling people how to be better, but helping them effectively achieve their own level of awareness and action."

—Wesley Warren, Director of Programs for Natural Resources Defense
Council, formerly Associate Director for the Office of Budget
and Management in the Clinton White House (1994-2001)

"Employee development is at the heart of every manager's job and, as Brian and Anne clearly demonstrate, coaching is the key to unlocking human potential. The authors help managers better understand the nature of their task by providing both practical guidelines and relevant examples and cases that bring their ideas to life. No matter how experienced, every manager has something to learn about improving performance, and those who adopt the coaching practices described in this book are certain to WIN BIG."

—Judi Brownell, Ph.D., Professor and Dean of Students,
School of Hotel Administration, Cornell University

"Anyone who manages people needs to read this book. It's full of practical advice, case studies, tips and proven systems for coaching employees to success. Our company is learning the important role that asking questions plays in overall success. This book unlocks that secret in a real, down-to-earth way."

—David Collins, President & CEO,
ARC (Airlines Reporting Corporation)

"Written in a breezy, easy-to-read format, this book offers managers, particularly those new to coaching, insights into how to get better results from direct reports. This book is the real deal. Seasoned beyond their years, Brian and Anne offer counsel that is both wise and practical to individuals at all levels of an organization."

—David Coleman, President,
Transitional Management Services

"The manager's guide is a sophisticated tool written in 'plain English.' This is a practical approach to the complicated challenges managers face in non-profit (or any) leadership [position]. Written with pervasive good humor and goodwill toward all, *The Manager's Guide to Coaching* makes workplace issues seem more interesting and less vexing."

—Craig Shniderman,
Executive Director, Food & Friends

"The coaching methods developed by Brian are among the most effective staff development tools in my management toolbox. The questioning techniques help create a supportive and solution-focused framework in what might otherwise be difficult conversations with struggling staff members. I even find the techniques effective in self-reflection on my personal performance."

—Charlotte Brantley, President and CEO,
Clayton Early Learning Foundation

"This book does a great job of presenting the model of coaching that has been very beneficial for me. I have worked with Brian for several years. The hours I've spent with him, being coached and learning to coach others, have been some of the most meaningful and valuable of my career."

—John Kyle, Vice President, Marketing, LogiXML

A MANAGER'S GUIDE TO COACHING

---■---

Simple and Effective Ways to Get the Best Out of Your Employees

Brian Emerson & Anne Loehr

American Management Association

New York • Atlanta • Brussels • Chicago • Mexico City
San Francisco • Shanghai • Tokyo • Toronto • Washington, D. C.

This publication is designed to provide accurate and authoritative information in regard to the subject matter covered. It is sold with the understanding that the publisher is not engaged in rendering legal, accounting, or other professional service. If legal advice or other expert assistance is required, the services of a competent professional person should be sought.

Library of Congress Cataloging-in-Publication Data

Emerson, Brian, 1967–
   A manager's guide to coaching : simple and effective ways to get the best out of your employees / Brian Emerson, Ann Loehr.
       p. cm.
   Includes index.
   ISBN 978-0-8144-0982-4
   ISBN 0-8144-0982-2
   1. Employees—Coaching of.   2. Employee motivation.   3. Problem solving.
I. Loehr, Ann.   II. Title.
HF5549.5.C53E44 2008
658.3'124—dc22

                                                          2007045792

Printing number

10 9 8 7 6

Contents

Acknowledgments

To be a coach requires one to have a desire to see another succeed. In that respect, we have had many coaches in our lives to whom we are greatly indebted. Some have been supportive, some have helped us learn, and some have helped us time and time again to overcome the hurdle that is ourselves. To all of them, we say thank you for the role you played in not only shaping this book, but in shaping us as well. To name them all would be an impossible feat, but there are some who deserve special mention in conjunction with this project.

Thank you to our clients (individuals and organizations) with whom we learn and in whom we believe.

Thank you to our colleagues and partners in learning—especially David Coleman, Amy Levine, Chuck Miller, Leah Rampy, Lisa Silverberg, and Jerren Pellicano for their input, review, and assistance in completing this work.

Thank you to Grace Freedson and Christina Parisi our agent and editor, respectively, who guided us through this new and exciting experience.

Thank you to our parents, siblings, nieces, and nephews who have coached and loved us unceasingly throughout the years.

Finally, thank you to Ariana, Neel, and Stephen for their unending support of this project and of us as people. We hope you know that we believe in you just as much as you believe in us.

1

Getting the Best from Employees

If you're not growing, you're dying.

It's a basic rule of life here on earth and in the business world today. It's what drives most of us to be better at what we do and who we are. It's the desire to "be more." Because of this desire, the term "coaching" has caught the attention of both the personal-growth and business worlds, creating a multibillion-dollar-a-year industry and a situation in which everyone wants a coach. More than ever, employees are asking for developmental opportunities and managers are being told they need to "coach" their employees on a regular basis. We've even worked with managers who say they've been told to "stop managing and start coaching." This all sounds great in theory—managers coaching employees to grow and be more effective—but there's one problem. Although many people agree that having a coach is a great way to move toward success, very few people know what a coach actually is or what a coach actually does. This leaves many managers scratching their heads as they try to fit one more ambiguous task into their already over-busy schedules.

So what is a coach, and what is coaching? This is our definition: A coach is someone who helps another person reach higher effectiveness by creating a dialogue that leads to awareness and action. By creating the space to step back, look in the mirror, and grapple with the tough questions, a coach helps a person examine and deal with their reactions to obstacles and, in a sense, "get out of their own way" as they achieve better results, in a more efficient manner.

But why is this important? Why is helping a person deal with their own personal obstacles so necessary? Why can't people just focus on the task at hand and put all that other emotional stuff to the side? The answer, much to the chagrin of many people and managers, is that as humans, we don't have a choice. If we are going to grow, be more, and reach higher levels of effectiveness, we have to spend time learning how to clear one of the biggest hurdles of success—our own emotional baggage.

THE SUCCESS EQUATION

When we are faced with a task (in business, or any aspect of life), there are three things that we need to be as successful as possible:

- **Aptitude**—the know-how, skills, and capacity to complete the task at hand
- **Attitude**—the drive, confidence, focus, and determination to complete the task at hand
- **Available Resources**—the tools, equipment, and time needed to complete the task at hand

Without these three components, we cannot be at the top of our game. The degree to which each of them does or does not exist directly contributes or detracts from our ultimate level of success. It can be thought of as an equation with variable components.

Aptitude	+	Attitude	+	Available Resources	=	Level of Success

- Know-How
- Skills
- Ability

- Drive
- Confidence
- Focus
- Enthusiasm

- Tools
- Equipment
- Time

Low Medium High

Start with Aptitude, the most obvious component of the equation. Without the proper skills and know-how (Aptitude) to complete a task, we are left scratching our head and frustrated. Think of a kid on her birthday receiving her first shiny, new bike. She has the determination and excitement (Attitude) to ride her new wheels (Available Resources), but she lacks the skill and ability (Aptitude) to go whizzing down the street as she envisions. After two or three wipeouts, you end up with a frustrated little birthday girl.

> The terms Aptitude and Attitude are not perfect descriptors and mean more here than in their traditional definitions. Aptitude is about more than someone's innate talent, and talking about someone's Attitude is about more than someone's positive or negative attitude.

Just as crucial to the equation is having the Available Resources to complete the task. Think of the last time your team at work had a great idea or new approach to accomplishing success—but you lacked the budget, time, or people power to execute it. You had the capacity to figure out a new solution (Aptitude), the drive and confidence to make it a reality (Attitude), but lacked the money or people (Available Resources) to pull it off. Not a fun place to be in, by any stretch of the imagination.

As managers, and people, we are comfortable and see the need to focus on Aptitude and Available Resources. When things aren't working in the office, managers are often very willing to train people in new skills or throw more money at the problem. However, it's the middle part of the Success Equation—the keystone if you will—that most people tend to overlook, forget about, or outright ignore. Attitude refers to things like the drive, confidence, focus, chutzpah, enthusiasm, grit, determination, need, desire, fortitude, and inspiration to accomplish the task at hand. Although difficult to measure and manage, without the right Attitude, having only the Aptitude and Available Resources will get you nowhere. Unfortunately, managers often say things like, "why can't people just do their jobs and leave all that other stuff at home." Well, people don't "leave all that other stuff at home" because as humans, we can't. Understandably, many managers wish that this was not the case, because managing would be immensely easier if people could really "check their emotions at the door." We get it, and, unfortunately, it's not possible. Think of the times your work day has been affected because you were ill, or you had a fight with a family member. This doesn't even include the events that happen at work. When rumors of a downsizing start in an organization, how many people are able to completely check their emotional reaction to the news and focus 100% on their work? Not many. So, for better or worse, managers have to accept that our Attitude affects our Level of Success, and focusing on it is more than "a nice thing to do." Like it or not, Attitude is hardwired into the Success Equation for humans, and not just as a variable on the periphery. Attitude is perhaps the most vital component in the entire equation, and focusing on it is a manager's business imperative.

Hardline business people are often most comfortable thinking of this in terms of sporting analogies. Anyone who has played sports has probably been told at one time or another to "get your head in the game," "focus," "get psyched up," or "don't think that you can't

> *Champions aren't made in the gyms. Champions are made from something they have deep inside them—a desire, a dream, a vision.*
> —Muhammad Ali, American Boxer
> http://www.famous-quotes-and-quotations.com/sports-quote.html

beat these guys!" Sports coaches know that the confidence, drive, and determination (the Attitude) of their athletes can make all the difference between playing and winning.

When a consistent athlete has a "bad day," we say they were "off their game" or that they "completely psyched themselves out." But what's changed in the Success Equation? They have the same skills and ability that they had when they won the game last week. Assuming that they are healthy, rested, physically fit, and that their equipment is in working order, then the variable in the equation has to be the athlete's Attitude—their focus, confidence, determination, or desire.

Aptitude	+	Attitude	+	Available Resources	=	Level of Success
• Know-How		• Drive		• Tools		Low Medium High
• Skills		• Confidence		• Equipment		
• Ability		• Focus		• Time		
		• Enthusiasm				

As Attitude shifts and drops, the result is a shift in the level of success—and this decrease can be the difference between winning and losing.

Good sports coaches know that the key to working with top athletes is focusing on the Attitude piece of the success equation—not because "focusing on this stuff makes people feel good and is a nice thing to do," but because the Level of Success depends on it. Attitude is the keystone in the success equation that can affect the Level of Success in exponential ways. Let's examine three of the reasons why this is true and how managers get in trouble by ignoring the Attitude component of the equation.

- Improved Attitude can compensate for deficiencies in Aptitude or Resources.
- A decrease in Aptitude or Resources often negatively affects Attitude, which can further hinder the Level of Success.
- The converse of the above is not true—A negative Attitude does not decrease the level of Aptitude or Resources.

Let's take a look at each of these individually.

Improved Attitude can compensate for deficiencies in Aptitude or Resources.

The first point above is what leads some to say that Attitude is the make-or-break factor of the success equation. Think of the multiple stories of athletes who have suffered an injury but upped their determination and grit to produce highly successful results. Kerri Strug, the gymnast in the 1996 Olympic Games who completed (and nailed) her final vault with two torn ligaments in her ankle is a perfect example—and there are thousands of others. This rule holds true outside of the sports world as well—it's evident in all aspects of our life and the business world. When faced with a lack of Aptitude or Resources, people will often "dig deep" to find the extra determination they need to win in a big way. Viewed in this manner, it is unarguable that Attitude is a central, and powerful, part of the success equation.

A decrease in Aptitude or Resources often negatively affects Attitude, which can further hinder the Level of Success.

Attitude is the only piece of the success equation that is directly affected by a shift in the other two components. Suppose John is leading a successful project at work.

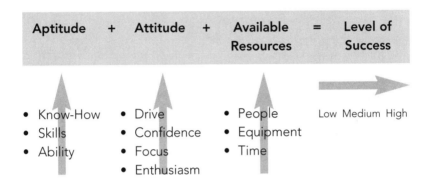

He has a high level of Aptitude and Attitude and is utilizing the Available Resources that he needs to reach a high level of success. Then, as is often the case, something changes. Assume that John loses two people on his team and finds out that the project deadline has been moved up a month earlier because of client demands. Obviously, fewer people and less time affect the Available Resources part of the equation, which in turn lowers the Level of Success.

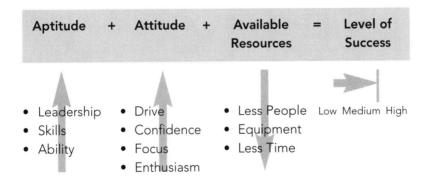

What is interesting about the Attitude component of the equation is the degree to which it is affected by a shift in the other components. As the project continues with increasing time pressure and fewer people power, it is understandable that John could become more frustrated and less confident in the success of the project. At the very least, he has more to do with less bandwidth which results in less focus. This shift in Attitude could further hinder the overall success of the project.

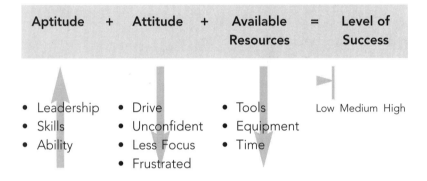

Aptitude	+	Attitude	+	Available Resources	=	Level of Success

- Leadership
- Skills
- Ability

- Drive
- Unconfident
- Less Focus
- Frustrated

- Tools
- Equipment
- Time

Low Medium High

Shifting Available Resources can directly affect Attitude. The same holds true with Aptitude. Think back to the example of the birthday girl and her new bike. She lacks the skills and know-how to ride the bike, and as a result, she is frustrated and unconfident. Now, before she can really learn the skills she needs to ride the bike, she has to overcome her frustration and be confident enough to try again. The same holds true for adults in the workplace. When an employee lacks the skills and ability to complete a certain aspect of a task, chances are their confidence and level of frustration will also be affected in the process. Thus, the ultimate Level of Success is affected in an exponential manner.

The converse of the above is not true—A negative Attitude does not decrease the level of Aptitude or Resources.

The third point outlined above is as vital as the first two. Assume Ariana is a highly skilled and focused employee who experiences high levels of success in her job.

Aptitude	+	Attitude	+	Available Resources	=	Level of Success

- Talented
- Skilled
- Smart

- Driven
- Confident
- Motivated
- Focused

- Tools
- Equipment
- Time

Low Medium High

One day, rumors begin to swirl that a downsizing is going to take place in the next 9–12 months and Ariana hears through the grapevine that her position will be eliminated. These rumors obviously change the success equation—but in only one area—Attitude. Ariana's drive, confidence, and focus may be negatively affected by the situation, which may decrease her level of success.

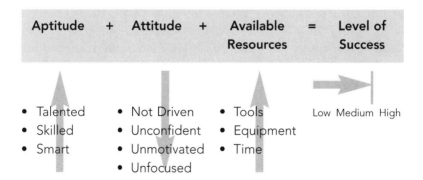

Aptitude	+	Attitude	+	Available Resources	=	Level of Success

- Talented
- Skilled
- Smart

- Not Driven
- Unconfident
- Unmotivated
- Unfocused

- Tools
- Equipment
- Time

Low Medium High

However, unlike the previous example of John, this impact or shift in the Attitude component of the equation does not, in any way, affect the other components of the equation. Ariana's dip in Attitude does not lower or change her Aptitude or her Available Resources. Additionally, unlike the athlete who can compensate for a lower part of the equation by upping his Attitude, as long as Ariana's Attitude is negatively affected, there is nothing that additional Aptitude or Available Resources can do to raise her Level of Success.

Again, Attitude is the keystone in the success equation.

All of these factors combined make learning how to improve someone's Attitude an extremely important skill. Managers need to be aware of, work to manage, and learn to develop the Attitude (the determination, motivation, focus, drive, confidence) of their employees.

> An employee having a "high" Attitude can affect their Level of Success in a very positive way. As a manager, look for the good parts of people's Attitude and find ways to help them capitalize on it.

We work with many managers who respond at this point by saying something like, "Yeah, but why do I need to take the time to worry about coaching my employees? I have enough on my plate already, and this coaching fad is a time-intensive process that doesn't directly contribute to the bottom line."

If you think you don't need to be coaching as a manager, think again. As a manager, one of the most important business imperatives you have is managing and developing the talent of your organization. If you don't, chances are that talent will go elsewhere, which costs your organization a lot of money. The cost to replace an employee is higher than you might think—up to 1.5–2 times their annual salary. Think about it, the money adds up—the lost productivity as the person is leaving and while the position is vacant, the time and money associated with recruiting, interviewing, and other human resources functions, and finally, the cost of lost productivity as a new person is trained and gets up to speed. All of this plus there is quite a good chance that the new employee will not even work out!

Poor management results in huge costs to an organization. A disturbing truth for managers is that most of the time, when people quit their jobs, they are *not* leaving an organization; they are leaving their manager. Research has shown that the most common reason employees leave a company has to do with their relationship with their immediate supervisor.[1] As much as organizations don't like to admit it, people leave as a direct result of something that their manager is, or is not, doing.

Another reason people leave their job is lack of developmental opportunities. People *want* to be developed. Gen X-ers (born after 1965) and Gen Y-ers (born between 1981 and 1995) consistently cite "the opportunity to develop" as one of the key indicators of job satisfaction, and they consistently turn to their managers for that opportunity. Charlotte Shelton and Laura Shelton, authors of *The NeXt Revolution,* asked 1,200 Gen-X employees to rank, in order of importance, their most important job characteristics. The top three characteristics were positive relationships with colleagues, interesting work, and continuous opportunities for learning.[2] They want to be exposed to new things that push their boundaries and make them more employable in the future. For this to happen, and for these employees to reach high Levels of Success, managers must be tuned

[1]CareerBuilder.com, "How to Cope with a Problem Boss," http://edition.cnn.com/2006/US/Careers/07/26/cb.hate.boss/index.html (accessed July 26, 2006). © Copyright CareerBuilder.com 2005. All rights reserved.

[2]Fisher, Anne, "What Do Gen Xers Want?" *Fortune* (January 20, 2006). http://money.cnn.com/2006/01/17/news/companies/bestcos_genx/index.htm.

in to not only increasing the Aptitude of these employees, but they must also be keenly aware of and help develop the Attitudes of these employees as well. If employees are really going to develop and excel, their managers must help enhance their confidence, motivation, determination, energy, and focus as they learn increasingly complex skills.

When broken down, it's hard to refute the fact that taking the time to manage and develop the talent of one's employees is a critical business imperative for managers of *all* levels. To do so, one must focus on the entire Success Equation—Aptitude, Attitude, and Available Resources. Because Attitude is the keystone of success, to effectively develop their employees, managers have to coach. Think of it this way:

- Employees want to be developed and look to their manager for that development.
- If they don't get it, they will leave that manager and be hired elsewhere.
- Each time this happens, poor managers cost the organization hundreds of thousands of dollars, which most organizations don't have to throw away.
- Therefore, managers have a business directive to develop their employee talent within an organization.
- Developing employees cannot happen unless a manager focuses on increasing the employees' Aptitude *and* Attitude.
- The Attitude component of the Success Equation is best developed through coaching.

Because of this, we believe the question is not, "Why should I waste my time and resources by focusing on coaching?" The real question is, "How can I *not* waste my time and resources?" The answer: "By focusing on coaching."

If you still think that Attitude doesn't play that big of a role in people's day-to-day work life, think through these examples.

- You have the skills to do the job, but due to the recent downsizing you have almost double the work to accomplish. Due to the positive relationship you have with your boss, you are very committed to the job. You are determined to excel and motivated to make your group look good. Will you be successful? Probably. More than likely, your higher Attitude is affecting your Level of Success despite the lack of Available Resources. Even if you are not 100% successful due to the downsizing, you will have a higher level of success than someone in the same situation who is not motivated, unfocused, and uncommitted to the job.

- Your team lands a huge, highly-competitive account that brings a new level of prestige to your firm. The new client loves all of your proposed ideas and tells you to think even bigger as you move forward. Everyone is extremely excited and motivated to get started even though you are down one team member due to an extended leave of absence. Is the pump primed for a successful project? Yes. Your team has the Aptitude, and a high Attitude as a result of the new client, which will more than compensate for the lack of Available Resources (due to the leave of absence),

> In addition to developing employees, coaching also increases productivity, satisfaction, and the amount of institutional knowledge retained as a direct benefit of the good management that results from supervisors learning to coach.

So what does all of this have to do with coaching? In short, coaching helps people raise the Attitude component of the Success

Equation. Again, our definition of coaching is helping another person reach higher effectiveness by creating a dialogue that leads to awareness and action. By creating the space to step back, look in the mirror, and grapple with the tough questions, coaching helps a person effectively deal with their reactions to the hurdles that are in their way as they move forward to achieve better results, in a more efficient manner.

USING THIS BOOK TO COACH SUCCESSFULLY

Effectively managing and developing the Attitude component of self and others is a vital skill for managers who want to be more successful, and coaching is the best way of doing that. Most average managers are capable of increasing an employee's Aptitude and finding Resources for their ultimate success. The difference between an average manager of people and a star manager lies in the one's ability to move people to higher levels of success *when something is affecting their Attitude* (drive, confidence, focus, determination, and/or energy). This is where the skill of coaching comes in.

Coaching focuses on the Attitude part of the Success Equation. It helps employees clarify what they really want to achieve and how to achieve it. After raising this awareness, coaching moves employees to action as the coach helps inspire them to strategize, plan, and hold true to their commitments.

There is incredible power in working with a coach, both in business and in real life. We have seen the shifts that occur in people's lives as a result of coaching. We have seen people achieve incredible things and get what they really want. We have seen, and experienced for ourselves, the ways in which coaching helps people "be more"—more successful, more productive, more fulfilled, and finally, more alive.

Often, the best coaching is from an external source because they're objective observers. However, we know that hiring an outside coach is not always possible and most of the time people have to rely on their manager, a friend, or even themselves for coaching. That's where this book comes in. Whether you are an individual who is trying to get clear on the next steps forward or a manager who is being told that you need to coach your employees to be successful, this book will help.

So, that's the purpose of this book. Coaching takes time, and time is money. Whether you are investing time in coaching your employees, or taking time out of your busy schedule to self-coach your way through a challenging issue, you want to be sure you are getting the biggest return on your investment. This book can be used in a number of different ways to help that happen:

- As a resource to learn how to successfully coach employees and colleagues
- As a resource to give to employees to kick-off and support (not replace) the coaching, when your time is limited
- As a resource for groups or teams as they grapple with a particular problem, situation, or question
- As a tool to coach yourself through different situations

The book is not necessarily meant to be read cover to cover. The first four chapters are laid out as a "how-to" on coaching. The following sections are groups of questions that will inspire your thinking and creativity as you move forward in either coaching your team or in your own growth. This book is meant to be a resource— a tool to help managers and individuals as they strive to achieve greater results, and continue growing. Remember, if you're not growing, you're dying. We believe most people choose the former.

2

The What, Why, and When of Coaching

We are the first to admit that managing people has never been, and will never be, easy. Most people don't dream of being a manager. Ask kids what they want to be when they grow up—they might say a doctor, an inventor, an astronaut . . . ; few will say, "a manager." However, to advance in one's career usually means a promotion that brings with it the job of managing others. An accountant becomes a Sr. Accountant overseeing an account team, a market specialist becomes a Regional Director with a field staff, and a bioengineer receives a promotion to manage an entire lab. After the initial thrill of the promotion wears off, people realize how complex managing others can be. That's because managing others is a big job that often comes with many thankless duties and responsibilities. Couple this with the fact that nowadays, in addition to managing, managers are expected to *develop* their employees, and you have a double-whammy. Developing oneself is challenge enough; determining how to effectively develop others is a massive job that requires many unique skills, talents, and tricks of the trade.

A good manager must master the use of a number of different tools and know when each is appropriate and when it is not. Coaching is just one of these skills. We don't want to give the impression that if a manager spends all of their time coaching, life will be dandy. Nothing could be further from the truth. An effective manager needs to know how and when to use the tool of coaching and when to pick another, more appropriate tool. There is an old adage that says, "When the only tool you have is a hammer, everything looks like a nail."

Well, let's take the metaphor just a bit further. Suppose you go into your bathroom one day and your toilet is leaking. Drip, drip, drip—water is making its way to the floor. Knowing that you need to fix the leak, you run for your toolbox. As you open it, you ask yourself why in the world you even bought a toolbox, because you only have one tool—a hammer. You look at the hammer and pause, wondering how you'll be able to use it to fix a toilet . . . but drip, drip, drip . . . you can hear water landing on the bathroom floor. Regardless of the fact that you've never actually seen anyone repair a toilet with a hammer, you grab it, and in your desperation, you run to the bathroom. You look at the leak, hold the hammer firmly, wind up, and WHACK! You hit the problem right on the head and are completely shocked when your drip, drip, drip turns into a gushing, splashing mess. A little farfetched, maybe . . . but how many times have you seen managers swoop in and try to "fix a little drip" with a heavy-handed approach that leaves things worse than they were before? They step back, wind up, and WHACK! They turn everything into a mess. Managers need a variety of tools in their well-appointed toolbox—and they need to know how to diagnose which situations call for which of their approaches.

We are the first to admit that coaching is not the only, or necessarily the best, management tool. However, when used appropriately in the right situation, coaching is a surefire way of developing and managing the people who report to you. So, before deciding to purchase one for the toolbox, a manager needs to know:

- What the tool of coaching actually is and does
- Why it works and belongs in a manager's toolbox
- When, and when not, to use the tool
- How to effectively use the tool

In this chapter, we examine the first three bullets above—the What, Why, and When of coaching. Chapter 3 is devoted completely to the How of coaching, and the remainder of the book is set up with tools to help you coach effectively so that you can become a talented user of this management skill that is more than just the latest fad.

WHAT IS THE TOOL OF COACHING?

As we said, coaching is not the end-all-and-be-all of management tools. Employees need coaching when they are experiencing problems with the Attitude (motivation, confidence, energy, focus, determination) component of the Success Equation. Good indicators of a coaching situation are things like:

- when a person is experiencing trouble completing a job that they should already know how to do (i.e., there is no Aptitude issue),
- when a person has gotten themselves completely wrapped around the axle about a certain situation, or
- when a person needs help dealing with the frustration they experience because they do not have the resources needed to complete the task at hand.

As humans, when we are in these situations, it is natural to need help getting ourselves out of the weeds. We need someone or something to help get us to a place where we can see things clearly and make solid decisions from a position of effectiveness and empowerment instead of a place where we are completely hung up and not seeing straight. That's where coaching comes in. Managers should use coaching as a tool when an employee has the skills and ability to do the specific task, but for some reason they are struggling with the confidence, focus, motivation, drive, or bandwidth to deal with the situation in a manner that is as effective as possible.

Much to the dismay of many managers, Attitude issues usually far outweigh Aptitude issues. Try this experiment:

- Think about your employees and the colleagues around you.
- Take a minute and make a list of the types of things that they spend the majority of their time struggling with.
- Examine the list.
- How many things on the list have to do with Aptitude—not having the skills and abilities to do the tactical aspect of their jobs?
- How many have to do with motivation, frustration, energy, focus, confidence, interpersonal issues—the intangible things that have nothing to do with the actual skill of completing the job at hand (the "Attitude" part of the Success Equation)?

Usually, the majority of items on such a list involve Attitude—the keystone in the Success Equation that affects the Level of Success in exponential ways.

If managers want their employees to be effective, they need to be able to help them deal with all of the things that are in the Attitude grouping from the exercise above. Coaching is about providing the support and guidance necessary to do just that.

Again, our definition of a coach is someone who helps another person reach higher levels of effectiveness by creating a dialogue that leads to awareness and action. Sounds good, huh? But what does it really mean and how does that help develop employees in the situations identified above?

Let's break it down.

Dialogue. A dialogue is a conversation in which both parties are seeking understanding. They are not trying to prove, teach, or motivate the other to do something. Coaching is a conversation in which the coach attempts to understand, and thereby help the coachee to understand, what and how it is that the coachee is blocking their own success. A coach "creates" this dialogue by using skills such as listening, asking, and others outlined in Chapter 3, and by focusing on helping the other person.

Helpful. There has to be a genuine concern for the coachee on the part of the coach. To be effective, a manager has to really want to see the employee succeed, and they must hold the belief that their own success is connected to the success of the employee. A certain level of trust must exist and the coach cannot be in a situation whereby they are trying to "fix it." This is tough. For the most part, managers are where they are in life because they are good at fixing things. They are so used to fixing problems, that they often don't put themselves in the role of helping other people fix it for themselves.

Awareness. The reason that a coach or manager does not try to "fix it" when they are coaching is because people learn more when they figure things out for themselves, especially when they are learning about *how* their Attitude is hindering their level of success. People learn more when they can be involved in their own teaching, and they are much more likely to take action on that teaching and apply it again in other situations if they have discovered it for themselves.

Action. At the end of a coaching dialogue, there is action of some sort. The coachee will do something differently, shift the direction of a goal, or try a new approach to their situation. Without action, the dialogue is just a nice conversation between an employee and a concerned manager, not coaching.

Higher Level of Effectiveness. The goal of the entire coaching process is to lead to higher levels of effectiveness. This is important to keep in mind, because coaching is not a quick-hit tool. It takes time, has a laid-back pace, and usually requires a manager to stop what they are doing and focus completely on the employee and the coaching situation. The good news to all of this is that when done correctly and in the right situation, coaching works to make the job of the manager easier because it develops employees who are learning and looking for new and better ways of doing their jobs and meeting company objectives in a timelier manner.

> Coaching is *not* just a nice way of teaching someone something. Teaching involves the direct transfer of skills and knowledge. Coaching involves helping another person gain the confidence, motivation, and drive to complete the task at hand.

So, coaching is helping another person reach higher levels of effectiveness by creating a dialogue that leads to awareness and action. Said differently, coaching is a two-way conversation in which a manager asks questions and provides support in a way that enables an employee to understand how they can make changes to be more effective for themselves, their manager, and their organization.

Why Does the Tool Work?

We hope that it is becoming more clear what exactly coaching is. But what makes it a good management tool, and why is it needed to meet the goals of developing employees? The answer, in short, is because coaching focuses on Awareness and Action, which are the

Table 2.1. *Another Look at "What Is a Coach?"*

Our Definition	What It Means
A coach is someone who	A coach is someone who
helps another person	has concern for another person and wants to see them
reach higher levels of effectiveness	be better in all areas of their work, so they
by creating a dialogue	engage the person by asking questions, listening, and being supportive in a way
that leads to awareness	that helps the person discover for themselves the ways in which their Attitude is hindering their Level of Success so that
and action.	the person can do something differently to be more effective in all areas of their work and life.

two key tenets in Emotional Intelligence. Emotional Intelligence has quickly become recognized as one of the most important indicators of how successful someone will be in business and in life. *Emotional Intelligence is awareness of one's thoughts and feelings as well as those of others so that one can take the appropriate actions to manage oneself in a way that gets the most out of every interaction.* Said more simply, Emotional Intelligence is knowing and managing your own buttons and triggers, as well as knowing and managing how you push the buttons of others. Awareness and Action are the building blocks of emotional intelligence—being aware and taking the most appropriate action to meet the goal.

Because of the word "emotional" in the term Emotional Intelligence, many managers want to write it off, saying, "This is the workplace, check your emotions at the door." But here's the news-flash—research has shown that the concept of checking one's emotions at the door is impossible and that the best and most successful employees learn how to recognize, manage, and harness the power of the emotions that drive them. To do this, employees must be aware of what's going on inside themselves, and then take the appropriate action to manage it.

Awareness, therefore, is key, because without it the likelihood of taking the most effective action is slim. Think of a dashboard in a car. All of the dials and digits exist to give you a certain amount of awareness of what is happening with the car. The gas gauge, as one example, keeps you aware of how much gas is in the tank. If you weren't aware that the car was getting low on gas, why would you take action and put more gas in it? If we are not aware of the impact of our actions, thoughts, and feelings, then we have no reason to take action and start behaving any differently. As individuals, we spend most of our time in a reactive state. We do things and react to situations often without actually realizing why it is that we are behaving in a certain way or doing a certain thing. When we are aware of what is going on, and can see it clearly, we realize that we have a choice in how we respond.

Take Jed, for example. Jed knows how to give effective feedback. He knows how important feedback is to continuous improvement and will often talk about needing to "give so-and-so feedback." However, it's also important to Jed to have a tight team—one that functions well, gets along, and is seen in the company as the "team to want to be." As a result, Jed will often delay in giving feedback because he doesn't want to upset the dynamics of the team, and many times, Jed "forgets" to give the feedback until it is "too late," in his opinion. This lack of feedback actually negatively affects the team because they're not getting all the information they need to move forward. If Jed is like most people, chances are he doesn't even see the connection between these two things, because we are often too close to our own "stuff" to see it clearly. If Jed isn't aware that this is going on, then how can he choose to do something different-ly? If his manager says, "Jed, you need to get better at giving feed-back," Jed will probably think, "I give feedback just fine—when I talk to people they understand what it is that they need to do differ-ently." As a result, he would not choose to do anything differently.

Suppose, through a coaching conversation, Jed becomes aware that one of the things that gets in his way of giving feedback is his desire to have a strong team dynamic. He can then explore why *not* giving the feedback actually hinders the team and he can choose a different strategy for giving feedback in a timely manner, perhaps by building in a specific time for feedback during his weekly one-on-ones with all of his direct reports, which would actually enhance the team's performance.

We are willing to venture that 9 times out of 10, when an employee is having an issue at work in which they are not being as productive as possible, it is *not* because they do not possess the spe-cific skill set to get the job done. Most people know how to do their work, it's just that they let their Attitude get in the way of their per-formance. Think back to the lists that you made earlier in this chap-ter. How many of the things that people struggle with at work involve lack of skill to do the job at hand? Really, not that many when you stop and think about it. Most of the time, it's their Attitude that needs improvement. To change this, they need to be made aware of what's going on so that they can then choose to take action to cor-rect it. Awareness is the key to producing different, more productive actions. Coaching not only helps an employee discover for them-selves the things that are in their way, but it also leads them to action, which is essential.

Awareness for awareness' sake can be nice in life, but in the world of business, the key is action and effectiveness. Coaching ensures that

One of a manager's jobs when coaching is to help the coachee enhance their self-awareness. This, however, does not involve the manager using a baseball bat. They use questions (see below) to help the employee discover for themselves, which elicits a greater commitment to change.

an individual will really take some action once they have become aware of a situation, which is vital if things are ever going to be different.

Many times at this point, managers will say, "Yeah, but it's just easier to tell the employee how to do it differently —I don't have time for helping build awareness." We all want a quick solution, but people need to discover for themselves if they are actually going to implement change. You can tell someone what to do, but in the long run, unless you are developing their self-awareness and self-management, you are going to keep finding yourself in the same situation explaining the same things and then banging your head against the same wall. Like we said in the first chapter, the question is not, "Why should I waste my time coaching?" It is, "How can I not waste my time?" The answer is through coaching.

COACHING VERSUS THERAPY

"I'm a manager, not a therapist." That thought might be going through your mind right now. Typically, it pops up when we start to teach people that coaching can hit on the "emotional" side of issues. Here's the deal. Coaching is not therapy, nor should it try to be. Unfortunately, in our society, we have started to define any conversation connected with emotions as therapy. Therapy examines and tries to deal with or remove the impact of the root causes of people's "issues." Coaching, remember, looks at a person's motivation, focus, confidence, or chutzpah, and gets them to figure out how they will deal with that to be successful.

There is a basic rule in skiing—where you focus is where you go. If you focus on the tree, you will head toward the tree (not a good thing). If you focus downhill, you will head downhill. Now, imagine you are out skiing and you are standing at the top of a beautiful ski trail. One of the biggest differences between coaching and therapy can be explained this way. In therapy, you will focus on the trees—those things that keep the trail from being as wide and obstacle-free as possible. This can be a great thing—who doesn't like a nice wide trail to whiz down the mountain of life? So in therapy, you ski to the tree, and contemplate things, such as how it got there, when your parents helped you plant it, and how it shows up in your dreams. Then, if you are lucky, you will initiate a plan to remove that tree from the mountain, or at the very least, to uproot it to be planted a little farther off the trail. We believe that therapy can be a great gift, but it is not coaching. In coaching, you might glance at the trees, but the job of coaching is to keep you focused on the ski run. As we ski through life, it is easy to get distracted (often unconsciously) by things on the side of the trail, which draw our focus away from the goal. Remember the rule of skiing—where you focus is where you go. As we focus on the things on the side of the trail (consciously or unconsciously), we start to go in that direction. Because we are not focused on the slope, the efficiency of our ski run is diminished and we are kept from skiing as fast and skillfully as possible. Coaching allows people to notice the trees, but does not try to figure them out or remove them. It's as if a coach was saying to you, "Hey, what are you looking at? What do you have to do to stop focusing on that and get down the hill more quickly?"

That said, there is no doubt that just like therapy, coaching can occasionally get emotional. People sometimes get angry. People sometimes get scared. People sometimes get upset. That, however, does not make it therapy. Really good leaders understand that people are emotional beings, and they find constructive ways to harness the power of emotions for the good of the cause. Think of Martin Luther King, Jr. or Nelson Mandela. Both were leading people whose emotions ran the gamut: hurt, anger, sadness, fear—you name it. But neither man ever asked the people who looked to him not to feel those emotions. Instead, they both knew how to tap into those emotions and say to people, "That's an OK tree to have on your slope, but what do we have to focus on to get us down this hill in the best way possible?" Coaching helps managers do the same thing. Coaching allows mangers to use employees' emotions—which have great power and energy—to increase their focus on the end goal so that they can get down the slope more quickly, with less effort, and have a better run.

WHEN TO COACH AND WHEN NOT TO COACH

As we have said before, coaching is just one tool that a manager must use to be successful. Used in the right situation at the right time, coaching can make the life of a manager immensely easier. Conversely, a manager will end up extremely frustrated if they try to coach employees who need something else from their manager, whose situations do not call for coaching, or who flat out don't want to be coached. Learning how to recognize when and when not to coach is just as important as learning *how* to coach.

Coaching is a dialogue that leads to Awareness and Action. When an employee has the skills and ability to complete the task at hand, but for some reason is struggling with the confidence, focus, motivation, drive, or bandwidth to be at their best, coaching can help. Employees typically struggle because one of three things is in their way:

1. Skills and Abilities—They currently lack the skill or ability to complete the task at hand; this relates to Aptitude
2. Themselves—They currently lack the motivation, focus, chutzpah, confidence, or commitment to complete the task at hand; this relates to Attitude

3. Outside Factors—They currently are being affected by things that are largely outside their control, such as not having the Available Resources, changing market conditions, ineffective vendors and partners (internal and external), or poor relationships with various stakeholders and colleagues.

To Coach or Not to Coach?
When determining whether a situation requires coaching, think about the employee and the situation at hand and ask yourself the following questions

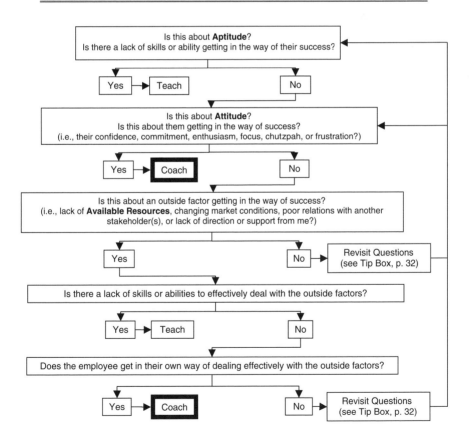

If an employee needs to develop specific skills and abilities, coaching is not the answer. You don't teach someone how to create a budget for the first time by asking them curious questions in an unattached manner! You teach someone a new skill by giving them the proper instructions for that particular task. If you tried to coach them, you would end up driving yourself crazy and your employee out the door. To that end, when determining whether coaching is the right tool to use in a certain situation, first ask yourself this question:

• Is this about Aptitude? Is there a lack of skills or ability getting in the way of the employee's success?

If the answer is "yes," then your answer to whether or not this is a coaching situation is "no." If an employee needs a certain skill set, your job is to find a way for them to learn those specific skills. Whether that be sitting down and teaching them, or setting up another type of training, you need to find a way for them to acquire the skills or the situation will never change.

If, in fact, the answer to the first question is "no" or "not really," next ask yourself:

• Is this about Attitude—their confidence, commitment, enthusiasm, focus, chutzpah, frustration?

If the answer is "yes," then you have a situation that is primed for coaching. You will want to create a dialogue that helps the employee become aware of what they are doing and then help them develop an alternative action that will lead to better results—in short, coach them.

If the answer to the second question is "no," then most likely the answer to the next, and final, question is "yes."

- Is this is about an outside factor getting in the way of success (i.e., lack of Available Resources, changing market conditions, poor relations with another stakeholder(s), or lack of direction or support from me)?

If the answer to this question is "no," you need to reevaluate the answers to all three questions because, chances are, you've missed something along the way (see the Tip Box, p. 32). If the answer is "yes," you have two more questions to ask yourself:

- Does the employee have the skills and abilities to effectively deal with the outside factors in order to be successful?
- Does the employee have difficulty dealing effectively with the outside factors despite having the skills?

The answers to these questions will lead you down the same path as before. If the employee needs skills, teach them, but be sure to do it while utilizing coaching skills such as concern and listening. If they need help with their attitude, coach them, but be prepared to offer suggestions and teaching tips along the way—dealing with outside factors can be tricky and there may be some skills you can teach as you go. Again, if the answer to both of these questions is "no," you should probably rethink the situation or better yet, have a conversation with the employee that focuses on the questions in the Tip Box on page 32.

All of this being said, the world is not a perfect place that follows the rules of flowcharts and authors. Many situations are not strictly about a problem with a singular component of the Success Equation (Aptitude, Attitude, and Available Resources). Often, it's a combination of two or three. The trick for managers is to be able to look at a situation and then use the right mix of teaching and coaching that is required to get the employee what they need. The

TIP   If answers to all of the Available-Resource questions seem to be "no" in your mind, ask the employee something like:

- It seems to me that "Project XX" is causing you a lot of angst. What would need to be different for you to say it was going smoothly?
- Talk to me a little bit about the situation with the "XX Team." How do you feel it's going?
- Fill me in on how you are doing with "XX"; what's working and what's not?

Listen to their answer(s). If it's about Aptitude and they need skills, teach them! If it's about Attitude, coach them!

case studies that follow offer good examples of how to handle situations that:

- Need a teaching conversation
- Need a coaching conversation
- Need a teaching conversation with some follow-up coaching
- Need a coaching conversation with a little teaching thrown in

Again, knowing when and when not to coach is vital. Remember the tool metaphor. Using a hammer to fix a leaking toilet can be disastrous—the toilet gets more damaged, the leak gets worse, and the "plumber" is left frustrated with a nasty mess to clean up. Take some time to read through the case studies that follow. They will help hone the skill of determining the coachability of different situations, which will keep you from cleaning up the bathroom floor later on.

TO COACH OR NOT TO COACH—CASE STUDIES

CASE #1 ■ LAURA AS PROJECT LEAD

The Scene
Technically speaking, Laura is one of the best people on your team. She is highly competent at what she does and is one of the most motivated and focused people you have ever worked with. Laura has been a key player on numerous project teams, and on many you have regarded her as your "number two." She knows what it takes to complete the types of projects you do, is respected by her peers, and always has great ideas and approaches that help your projects surpass their goals.

As a result of Laura's success, about a month ago, you decided to make her team-lead for the next project. You informed her of your decision and told her that although you would be a member of the team, she would be leading it—the goal being that after this project you would start to pull yourself completely out of the process. You then met with her about a week later to go over the project plan that she had created. You let her know that her approach was excellent, and you have no doubt that she was on her way to overseeing a successful project.

During the first two team meetings, a problem has arisen—the meetings are dreadful and, for the most part, a waste of time. There is no agenda (written or otherwise) and in addition to starting late, Laura has not been clear about what it is that she hopes to accomplish during the time that she has the team together, so people leave the meeting unclear of their next steps or responsibilities. Laura is apparently unphased by any of this and is following her project plan "to a T." You know you need to have a conversation with Laura about the meetings, and you are just beginning to think about how to proceed.

The Questions
1. Is this a situation that calls for coaching?
2. How would you structure the conversation?

The Response

1. Is this a situation that calls for coaching?

The first question to ask oneself is: Is this about Aptitude, Attitude, or Available Resources?

In this case, the question is about Laura's Aptitude in planning and running a meeting. Laura has the project management skills, but has no experience in conducting an effective meeting. This is not a situation for coaching, but rather for teaching. Laura needs to be taught some basic techniques for leading a meeting, and then perhaps help in implementing those techniques.

2. How would you structure the conversation?
   A. Tell Laura you want to check in on how the project is going.
   B. Ask her how she thinks everything is progressing.
   C. If she brings up the topic of her dreadful meetings, ask her if you can give her some feedback and go to E.
   D. If she doesn't bring up the topic of meetings, reassure her that you think her technique and plan are solid and then ask her if you can give her some feedback.
   E. Tell her your intent is to see her succeed and a way to do that is for her to make the most of the time she has the team together for meetings.
   F. Teach her about setting meeting objectives, outlining agendas, and assigning tasks with deadlines to people at the meeting.
   G. Ask her if she has any additional thoughts about how she might make the most of her meetings.
   H. Assure her of your confidence in her as a team lead and in the project.

CASE #2 ■ COLE AS CROSS-FUNCTIONING TEAM LEADER

The Scene

Cole is one of your star employees. He's risen quickly and has become a strong player within his own small team. He is ambitious, assertive, and can think outside of the box. He knows what it takes to lead a successful project team, and has done so many times. He is respected by his peers, as well as others in the company who want to duplicate his systems. His work is even beginning to gain the attention of the senior management team.

As a result of Cole's success and your desire to help him grow and develop, you assigned him to a new type of project: Leading a cross-functional project team, of which some members are more senior. You told Cole the good news. Surprisingly, he wasn't as excited as you had expected. However, he said that he'd gladly take on the new challenge and wouldn't fail. He requested that you meet with him later in the week to go over his project plan—a request that you found a bit odd, given his large amount of experience. As usual, the plan was well thought out; you let him know that he was on his way to leading another successful company project. You also let him know that you'd be attending the first few meetings as his support, but would eventually turn it completely over to him.

The first two meetings went well. Cole presented a clear agenda, defined roles succinctly, and ensured that everyone knew the objective and expectations of the project. However, at the third meeting, you noticed that when challenged, Cole deferred to the senior members of the team, instead of stepping up or taking charge of the situation. Then during the last meeting, a team member senior to Cole asked him to clarify one of his decisions. "Why did you decide X instead of going with Y?" To your surprise, Cole began to backpedal on his decision (which you thought was a sound one) and ended by saying, "You know, it's fine if we go with Y." Cole left the meeting a little shaken, and you left baffled about what had happened and why Cole wasn't stepping up to the plate like you thought he would.

You know you need to have a conversation with Cole about the project in general, and the last meeting in particular, and you are just beginning to think about how to proceed.

The Questions
1. Is this a situation that calls for coaching?
2. How would you structure the conversation?

The Response
1. Is this a situation that calls for coaching?
The first question to ask oneself is: Is this about Aptitude, Attitude, or Available Resources?

This situation is about Cole's Attitude toward successfully running a new project and leading senior members on the team. Cole has the project-management skills (Aptitude), but is lacking confidence (Attitude) when interacting with, or being questioned by, senior members of the project. This is a coaching situation because it is about Attitude. Cole is holding back and needs to be coached on his confidence level when interacting with senior members on the team.

2. How would you structure the conversation?
   A. Tell Cole you want to check in on how the project is going.
   B. Ask him how he thinks everything is progressing.
   C. If he brings up the topic of the senior members of the team, start coaching him on this topic. (See Chapters 3–7 on how to coach effectively.)
   D. If he doesn't bring up the topic of working with senior members of the team, reassure him that you think his skills and planning to date are very good and then ask him if you can give him some feedback and possibly do some coaching with him.
   E. Tell him your intent is to see him succeed and a way to do that is to provide the leadership, of which you know he is capable, to every member of the team—even those people more senior to him.
   F. Start coaching him on this topic. (See Chapters 3–7 on how to coach effectively.)
   G. Assure him of your confidence in him as a team lead and in the project.

CASE #3 ■ THOM'S DIFFICULT CONVERSATIONS

The Scene

Thom is one of your strong, solid employees. He gets the job done well and on time. He rarely causes waves in the department and can always be relied on. He doesn't say much, but when he does, everyone takes notice and listens, including you. He's good at working with a variety of people within his specialized field of accounting. He's been working with you for three years and you hope he will stay with you for another five years, as he's a solid keystone for the team.

Sue is an extroverted, assertive key player over in the sales department. She is a mover and shaker, who always wants to get things done ASAP. She can be quite vivacious and the life of the party. She brings in a majority of your sales quota every month. Sue doesn't pay attention to the details of accounting; she just sells and expects the finance department to handle the minutia.

Sue hasn't handed in her expense reports for the past few months. Thom asked her colleagues to remind her, but they were still missing. You've told Thom to deal with the situation, but Thom keeps asking others to ask Sue whether or not she has received his reminder e-mails. You've noticed lately that Thom's not as reliable as he used to be, and seems to be more frustrated with others than usual.

You know you need to have a conversation with Thom about his recent unreliability and frustration, as well as his unwillingness to talk to Sue directly to rectify the expense report problem. You are just starting to think about what the conversation will be like.

The Questions
1. Is this a situation that calls for coaching?
2. How would you structure the conversation?

The Response
1. Is this a situation that calls for coaching?
The first question to ask oneself is: Is this about Aptitude, Attitude, or Available Resources?

This case is about Thom's Attitude of unwillingness to face a potential conflict with Sue and the resulting general frustration and unreliability. This is a coaching situation because it is about Attitude. Thom is avoiding a potentially difficult conversation and needs to be coached on his unwillingness to face an issue head-on.

However, in addition, Thom may need some training on how to handle difficult conversations and conflict. It's possible that he doesn't know how to structure a conversation that involves some sort of conflict. If this is true, once he has these skills, his motivation may increase because his Aptitude will have improved.

So Thom needs coaching *and* training, to increase both his Aptitude and his Attitude. Basic conflict-management and difficult-conversation skill development are needed to improve his Aptitude. Coaching is needed to ensure that Thom has the motivation and confidence to learn and utilize the new skills. Your job is to teach Thom how to handle difficult conversations, while coaching his frustration and unwillingness to deal with conflict.

2. **How would you structure the conversation?**
   A. Tell Thom you want to check in on how work is going.
   B. Ask him how he thinks everything is progressing.
   C. If he brings up the topic of Sue, then start coaching him on this topic. (See Chapters 3–7 on how to coach effectively.)
   D. If he doesn't bring up the topic of Sue, reassure him that he is one of your most reliable employees and that you would like to talk a bit about the recent few weeks at work. Then ask him if you can give him some feedback and possibly do some coaching with him.
   E. Tell him your intent is to see him succeed and a way to do that is to successfully handle difficult conversations and face conflict head-on.
   F. Start coaching him on this topic. (See Chapters 3–7 on how to coach effectively.)
   G. Tell him that as part of the coaching follow-up actions, you'd like to help him with some training on difficult conversations. Start with some basic training, or set up a time for more skill development.

Many managers are uncomfortable using the term "coaching" or saying things like, "Do you want to do some coaching on the topic?" It is important to get the person's buy-in before coaching, so you can say things like, "Do you want to spend a few minutes batting some ideas around?" or "If you want, we could talk a bit about it to figure out how to make it stop driving you crazy."

H. Ask him if he has any additional thoughts on how he might improve his skills in this area, and point out the skills that you see he already has that will make him effective at having difficult conversations.

I. Assure him of your confidence in his ability to learn from the training and to successfully navigate difficult conversations in the near future.

CASE #4 ■ DENISE AND
THE DELINQUENT CLIENT

The Scene

Denise is a pure joy to work with. She has been successfully running projects for the past two years. Not only does she manage them effectively, but she has also started training other team members how to manage projects as well. She is very successful in time management, ensuring that all deadlines are met on time, if not early.

Recently, a new type of project came up. Because Denise is the "queen of projects," you naturally assigned Project X to her, assuming that she would manage this one as well as she managed others in the past. The project requires Denise to work with a client that your company has never worked with before, but Denise was unfazed by this information. She planned to work with this client just like she had worked with past clients. Because of your confidence in Denise's skills, you had no worries about her, or the project.

The first three meetings go well. Denise uses her usual style of project management with the new clients, outlining the key success factors, roles, responsibilities, and timelines. The new clients are impressed with her skills and promise to get all critical information to her in a timely manner.

The fourth internal meeting doesn't go as well. Two departments are complaining that they don't have critical information they need from the new client, which is creating a backup that threatens the timely production of deliverables. Denise promises to contact the client and get the information within twenty-four hours for the two departments. When called, the client apologizes for the oversight, and assures Denise it will never happen again. Yet, the information is not forthcoming within twenty-four hours, or even within the next four days, despite many calls from Denise. The client finally gets the information to Denise on day five, which forces the other departments to rush to do their work, inputting the late information. Denise is getting calls from the departments, complaining about the rush and giving Denise a hard time for making their lives so miserable. Denise is getting more and more frustrated by the situation, wishing she had never taken on Project X and other members of your department are starting to go out of their way to avoid her and her harried and sour attitude.

You are concerned because you know this project will go on for at least another year, and you are worried about how the situation with Denise will affect dynamics in your department and your relationship with other departments in the organization. You know you need to have a conversation with Denise, and you are just beginning to think about how the conversation will proceed.

The Questions
1. Is this a situation that calls for coaching?
2. How would you structure the conversation?

The Response
1. Is this a situation that calls for coaching?
The first question one should ask oneself is: Is this about Aptitude, Attitude, or Available Resources?

This case is about Denise's lack of control over her Available Resources. Denise has the project management skills, and started with the Attitude to do a good job, but has no experience in handling difficult clients who are constantly late, thus affecting her work and her team. Handling difficult clients is a new skill that she needs to learn, so she will need some training for this.

However, in addition to this skill development, Denise needs some coaching on her frustration with the client. Her irritation is showing to the client, as well as to her team and other people in your department. Although she may wish she had never taken on Project X, this type of situation will likely occur again, so coaching on her Attitude during these types of situations whereby things are "out of her control" would be useful for her future success.

So, Denise needs both coaching *and* training, to increase both her Aptitude and Attitude. Training in how to get the Available Resources she needs from difficult clients is needed to improve her Aptitude (imposing late fees, identifying clear decision makers, etc.). Coaching is also needed to ensure that Denise manages her frustration with the client, without letting it affect her team and other work. Your job is to teach her how to manage an untimely client while also coaching her on how to self-manage her frustrations when things happen outside her control. Teaching gives her the skills, but coaching gets her refocused and recommitted to the project.

2. **How would you structure the conversation?**
    A. Tell Denise you want to check in on how the project is going.
    B. Ask her how she thinks everything is progressing.
    C. If she brings up the topic of the new client being late and affecting the project, ask her if you can give her some feedback, and go to E.
    D. If she doesn't bring up the topic of the new client, reassure her that you think her technique and plan are solid and then ask her if you can give her some feedback.
    E. Tell her your intent is to see her succeed and that you understand how frustrated she must be, having to deal with a client who doesn't meet deadlines. Tell her you want to kick around some ideas about how to manage things that are out of her control so that it doesn't affect the people she is leading.
    F. Teach her about setting expectations with clients, writing client contracts with deadlines, enforcing those contracts if necessary, and how to have difficult conversations with clients.
    G. Then start coaching her on her frustrations with the client. (See Chapters 3–7 on how to coach effectively.)
    H. Ask her if she has any additional thoughts on how she might manage things that are out of her control.
    I. Assure her of your confidence in her as a team lead and in the project.

CASE #5 ■ MIKE AND THE MICRO-MANAGING BOSS

The Scene

Mike is a member of a cross-functoinal team that you lead. He does not report directly to you, but you have been his team leader for almost two years. During the past six months you have noticed a shift in Mike's performance on the team. He seems more withdrawn and although his work product was never spectacular, you have noticed a decline in the quality of what he produces for the team.

As you think back through the past months, you are sure that nothing has shifted on the team. Mike's roles and responsibilities have remained the same, and the team has been performing as usual.

In passing, you ask Mike how he is doing, and are surprised by his response. He tells you that he is going crazy working for Bess. She has been micro-managing him, he feels like he is not developing, and her gloom-and-doom attitude is really starting to wear him down.

The Questions

1. Is this a situation that calls for coaching?
2. How would you structure the conversation?

The Response

1. Is this a situation that calls for coaching?

The first question one should ask oneself is: Is this about Aptitude, Attitude, or Available Resources?

Mike's performance on your team has never been over-the-top. However, you know he does have the skills and the resources to at least complete the job. It would make sense, especially given the conversation about Bess, that Mike's Attitude is a major source of the problem. He is frustrated, and due to the micro-managing could possibly feel unconfident with his skills. So, Mike could definitely use some coaching.

As a leader, however, you want to keep an eye open for any skills Mike might need to up his Aptitude. He's never reached a really high level of success. Only through talking with him will you be able to determine how much of that is due to Attitude and how much might be due to some sort of deficiency in Aptitude.

2. **How would you structure the conversation?**
    A.   Since Mike brought it up, give him some feedback on the way you see his Attitude impacting his work on your team (withdrawing, etc.)
    B.   Assure Mike that he is a valuable team member and ask him if he wants to spend some time talking and brainstorming how to deal with the situation.
    C.   Start coaching him on the topic. (See Chapters 3-7 on how to coach effectively)
    D.   Be prepared to address any type of Aptitude issue that might arise by setting a time to teach and train.
    E.   Reaffirm your commitment to Mike as a member of your team and make yourself available for follow up.

Knowing what coaching is, why it works, and when to use it are all important pieces of information. Coaching is an invaluable tool for the manager to have in their toolbox, and many of the skills that make one a good coach are transferable to other aspects of management as well. Of course, having a tool does a person no good if they don't know how to use it. The remainder of the book focuses on how to coach and how to use coaching to get the best from your employees.

3

How to Coach and W.I.N. B.I.G.!

Imagine trying to teach someone to ski by only writing a book for them. That was the predicament we were in when we began the process of writing this book. Many people say that coaching, like skiing and good management, is more of an art than a science. There are many components and nuances that make up successful coaching, and trying to break them all down and lay them out for someone to pick up is tricky. To teach someone to ski through a book, you would have to outline a basic formula for success and then add tons of tips on all the intricate nuances it takes to be a good skier. That's what we've done in the remainder of this book. In this chapter, we take all that we discussed so far and outline our W.I.N. B.I.G. coaching formula. This basic formula for success will guide you through any coaching conversation in which you become involved. The following chapter is filled with tons of tips and practical suggestions to help you develop your flair and finesse when coaching—and in many other situations in life. The final chapters of the book contain hundreds of great questions and conversation starters for when you are coaching. Learning to ski by reading a book is possible, but difficult. We're convinced that by using the formula and tips in this book, your attempt at coaching will be much less painful and much more productive.

THE COACHING PROCESS

As we jump into "how to coach," it's important to remember two things:

1. Coaching is used when dealing with the Attitude component of the Success Equation (see When to Coach and When Not to Coach and Figure 2.1 in Chapter 2), and

Aptitude	+	Attitude	+	Available Resources	=	Level of Success

- Know-How
- Skills
- Ability

- Drive
- Confidence
- Focus
- Enthusiasm

- Tools
- Equipment
- Time

Low Medium High

2. To help enhance someone's Attitude, one must first help the person gain an awareness of what is going on and then move them to action by helping them devise different strategies.

It is upon these two components that our definition of coaching is built (see Table 2.1).

At a very high level, coaching has three parts. When you are coaching, you must first ask yourself whether this situation calls for coaching or for another tool in your management toolbox. In Chapter 2, we explained how important it is to Determine Coachability; this step is crucial. You will drive yourself and your employees crazy if you try to coach at the wrong time—just as you'll drive them crazy if you don't coach when you should. When, and only when, you have determined that the situation requires coaching can you move to part two of the coaching process.

The second aspect of coaching is to ask questions that create a dialogue to Build Awareness. As we said in Chapter 2, Awareness is the key to any personal change. If one is not aware of one's actions and the effect of those actions, then why or how should they change? Remember the example of a fuel gauge in your car: if you weren't aware that you were low on fuel, why would you stop to put gasoline in your car? As a coach, your job is to help the coachee become more aware of how they are getting in the way of their own success, and what they need to do to enhance the Attitude component of the Success Equation.

Of course, having someone become aware means nothing if they take no action. The third part of what you do as a coach is help the coachee Move to Action and then hold them accountable to their commitments. This ensures that the conversation you've had is actually a coaching conversation and not just a nice navel-gazing session.

The Coaching Process

Determine Coachability ➡ Build Awareness ➡ Move to Action

Certainly, there's a little more to it than what we've just laid out, but at a high level, that's what you're doing when you coach: determining whether the situation requires coaching, asking questions to create a dialogue that builds awareness about the issues at hand, and then moving the coachee to take action so that change will occur and the person will be more effective. Later in this chapter, we will outline in detail our step-by-step process of how to Build Awareness and Move to Action by using our W.I.N. B.I.G. formula. With it, you will know exactly how to coach someone through the stages above successfully and effectively. Before we do that, however, there is one part of the coaching process mentioned above that we want to examine more closely.

When describing the aforementioned Build Awareness phase of the coaching process, we were intentional about using the phrase "asking questions to create a dialogue that builds awareness." Questions are the backbone and lifeblood of a coaching dialogue, for they run all the way through the coaching process. Table 3.1 outlines some of the high-level questions that guide each stage of the coaching process.

Remember that a manager's job while coaching is not to fix anything, not to give advice, not to tell the employee what to do. The coach's job is to Build Awareness and Move to Action. The only way to do that is to ask questions that help the employee discover for themselves what it is that they need to be doing differently to stop hindering their own success. Because of the important role that

Table 3.1. *Questions That Guide the Coaching Process*

Stage of Coaching Process	Guiding Questions
Determine Coachability	Is this about Aptitude? Is this about Attitude? Is this about Available Resources?
Build Awareness	What's *really* going on? What does the employee want?
Move to Action	What will the employee do about it? How will I know?

questions have in the success of coaching, we want to explore the role of curiosity and the art of asking good questions, both crucial to coaching, before we examine the W.I.N. B.I.G. formula for coaching success.

COACHING QUESTIONS

One of the things that distinguishes a coaching dialogue from other conversations in the workplace (or life for that matter) is the amount and types of questions asked by the manager. It is not outside the realm of possibility for a coach to do nothing more than ask questions during a coaching conversation. This may sound odd in our information-overload culture in which everyone is taught that knowledge is power, but it's true. Coaching involves an employee's Attitude (confidence, determination, spirit, etc.) and there is only one person who can change anything about an employee's Attitude—the employee! To be effective, you can't tell a person how to feel, you can't give advice on motivation, you can't suggest that the person strengthen their backbone. The only way to help another person enhance their Attitude and thereby reach higher levels of effectiveness is by creating a dialogue that leads them to Awareness and Action. This dialogue is created *not* by telling, but by asking.

Think back to a time when you were nervously heading to a job interview. Your best friend said, "Don't worry, you'll be fine!" Miraculously, you felt better and the butterflies left your stomach en masse. Right? Whatever. How about the time you had to deliver really bad news to your boss? You thought you were going to get chewed out, or worse, fired. As you sat at your desk fretting, a colleague said, "Whenever I have to deal with him, I just look him in the eye and blurt it out. I don't worry about it. Just march in there and get it over with." Again, the weight on your shoulders lifted and you got up, full of confidence and calm, and marched into his office, right? Doubt it.

If you're like most people, being told by someone else how to change your Attitude doesn't work. We are all unique beings with different wiring and buttons. What works for one person doesn't necessarily work for another. To change an aspect of your Attitude, you have to discover it for yourself and follow the corrective steps that work for you. Other people's suggestions might be helpful, and they are usually well-intentioned, but they don't fix the problem. That's where questions come in and why they are so crucial to coaching.

Now, it would be too simple if all that a manager had to do to develop their employees was go out and ask some questions. There is a big difference between questions and coaching questions. Coaching questions open a dialogue—they are like keys that open doors to answers and possibilities for people. The keys allow people to look inside "rooms" and discover solutions and strengths that they may have never known existed. Asking good questions is what makes coaching possible and what ultimately leads to getting the most from your employees. Learning to ask good coaching questions is easy if you stay curious and if you focus on these five suggestions:

1. Keep them open
2. Keep them advice-free
3. Keep them short and simple
4. Keep them thought-provoking
5. Keep them forward-focused

Remembering these suggestions can help a coach ask stronger questions that more quickly Build Awareness and Move to Action. Let's take a look at each individually to examine the role it has in the coaching process.

Keep Them Open

Closed-ended questions don't usually provide real information. Most people know that they should avoid closed-ended questions, but, surprisingly, they ask them anyway. Closed-ended questions elicit an answer of yes or no, or at best one or two other words, such as "good," "fine," or "OK." They don't lead to a dialogue, let alone Awareness or Action.

> Starting questions with words such as "will," "did," and "have" will likely lead you into a close-ended question. Try to rephrase those questions to start with words such as "what," "who," and "how."

- Will the project be done on time?
- Did you check all of the requirements?
- Have you notified Sarah about the changes?

It's possible for each of these to be answered by one word, which may leave many stones unturned in terms of employee effectiveness.

Open-ended questions, however, open a conversation of exploration and understanding. They can't typically be answered in one or two words and require the responder to elaborate and share more information. They help create a fuller picture and raise awareness. Let's take the examples above and turn them into open-ended questions (see Table 3.2).

Table 3.2. *Creating Open-Ended Questions*

Closed-Ended	Open-Ended
• Will the project be done on time?	• What are the things that stand in the way of the project meeting its deadline?
• Did you check all of the requirements?	• Which of the requirements most concerns you?
• Have you notified Sarah about the changes?	• Who are the key players that you need to notify about the changes?

By asking a question more similar to the open-ended examples, not only would a manager get better information, but they might also help the employee think through an aspect of the situation that they would not have otherwise. The questions lead to more conversation that will most likely lead to higher levels of effectiveness. When coaching, especially when trying to Build Awareness, it is vital to ask open-ended questions that lead both the manager and employee deeper into conversation.

Keep Them Advice-Free

One of the biggest traps that managers who are learning to coach fall into is the old "advice disguised as a question" snare. These managers know that, in order to coach, they have to ask questions. So, they do that diligently. What they don't do, however, is let go of their need to fix it and give advice. They want to take the problem away from the employee and solve it. Unfortunately for the manager and the employee, this doesn't work.

Think about the conversations in your life in which you have talked to someone about a problem. How many times has someone said to you something like:

- Have you tried . . . ?
- Why don't you . . . ?
- What if you . . . ?

Our guess is that the 9 times out of 10 that someone started a "question" that way, you had already run that potential solution through your mind and determined why it wouldn't work. Very rarely are questions that start like the ones above met with an, "Oh, my gosh, that's exactly what I should do. Why didn't I think of that!?!"

When you are coaching someone, you can safely bet that they have thought through their situation *way* more than you have and

We can safely guarantee that when starting to coach as a manager you will be tempted to disguise advice as a question. If it happens, so be it. It's not the end of the world by any stretch of the imagination. However, when you are coaching, you have to be prepared, and OK with, having the person reject your advice. As a coach, you cannot be attached to the solutions you provide. See Be Unattached in Chapter 4 for more thoughts and tips.

they have come up with multiple solutions to the problem. They have also run each of those solutions through their internal "solution tester" and can tell you why each one won't work. Remember, if you are coaching, it is not because the person does not know how to solve the problem, it is because of emotional hurdles that prevent them from implementing the best solution. So, instead of "Have you thought about," try "What's the best solution to this in your mind?" and follow it up with, "What would it take to make that happen?"

Keep Them Short and Simple

In our experience, the most powerful coaching questions are often the shortest. Managers who are learning to coach often agonize over how to word eloquent questions (often disguising some sort of advice). They think that the art of coaching is in asking magnificently complex questions. Wrong. The art of coaching is staying curious about what is going on for the employee and really listening to what they are saying. If you are busy composing your next brilliant question, then you're not listening! When you take the time to really listen to what the coachee is saying, the right questions will come to mind. The questions in the back of this book can be helpful as well. At the end of a coaching conversation, an employee will not walk away remembering your beautifully phrased questions.

What they will remember is that you listened to them and they felt heard.

In reality, short questions often work best. Our rule of thumb is questions of 5–10 words are usually a good way to go. They typically come from a place of curiosity, are too short to be advice, and keep the coach focused on the employee. Examples are found in Table 3.3.

Keep Them Thought-Inspiring

As we have said before, when you are coaching someone on a particular topic, chances are the topic has consumed much of their bandwidth for a long time. Because of that, they have thought about possibilities, they have thought about causes, they have thought about everything, and they need you to help them think bigger. A great example often used in coaching circles is about teaching someone to kick a soccer ball. Asking them, "Are you keeping your eye on the ball as it comes toward you?" will elicit a "yes" or "no" that doesn't help them see the situation in a new light. However, asking

Table 3.3. *Short versus Long Questions*

Long	Short
• In the end, if it could go perfectly in your mind, how would you like everything to work itself out?	• What do you want?
• So, tell me how you see that playing out and what kind of effect do you expect it to have on the project?	• What will that get you?
• Are you letting your concern over the numbers outweigh your desire to have everyone on the team get along?	• What's stopping you?

a question like, "As the ball comes toward you, which way is it spinning?" or "Do you see more black or more white on the ball as it approaches?" or "How many times does the ball bounce before it gets to you?" will help them to look at the situation differently and ensure that they are keeping their eye on the ball. Likewise, if you are coaching an

> If you ever get stuck and seriously can't think of a question, say "I'm not sure what to ask. What question should I be asking you?" Most of the time, the person will ask a question that moves them to a new level of awareness or action.

employee who is struggling with leading a dysfunctional team and ask, "Is your team getting along?" you will get a "yes" or "no" answer and shed no new light on the situation. However, questions like, "What are the times your team has the lowest energy?" or "How do your team members feel about the end goal?" or "If your team was a TV show, what would it be?" all make the employee assess the team a little differently, thus making new approaches and solutions possible.

Keep Them Forward-Focused

In general, when coaching, you want to keep the coachee forward-focused. It can be really easy to get caught in the cycle of replaying and rehashing meetings and events, talking about the blow-by-blow of what happened. As a manager, that can sometimes be important, but as a coach who is trying to enhance an employee's Attitude to increase their effectiveness, it is more useful to keep the conversation forward-focused. One of the ways people's Attitude is affected is by replaying past events. As a coach, you want to help the employee step back from the events, learn from them, and then focus forward. It's like the skiing example we used before: where you focus is where you go. When employees are busy looking at the trees (or back up the hill!), you need to gently nudge them to be forward-focused on the slope. Undoubtedly, people often need to vent and work through some of their emotions before they are ready to look forward. That's completely understandable, and as a coaching manager, you want to let them do that for a few minutes. However, your job is to ensure that they don't get stuck in the venting and that they eventually begin to look forward to a place of more effectiveness (Table 3.4).

Table 3.4. *Coaching Requires Keeping Employees Forward-Focused*

Employee Response	Typical Manager Responses That Stay Stuck in the Past	Forward-Focused Question
The meeting I just ran was a fiasco . . . (*details, details, details*)	What happened then? Did you have the handouts of the project plans?	How do you want your meetings to run? What do you need to do differently for that to happen?
I can't believe I just let her get to me like that!	What did she say when you . . . ? Why didn't you tell her . . . ?	How would you like to be when she's like that? What do you need to do to keep centered next time?
The whole project has been a mess, we are . . . (*details, details, details*)	What did you do about marketing? Why haven't you contacted IT?	What are the things you need to do to bring it back on track? What do you need to do to keep your eye on the finish line?

One of the biggest, and most important, ways that you can keep people forward-focused is to avoid questions that begin with "why" when you coach. When we ask someone a question that starts with "why," they are immediately placed in a position where they have to defend what it is that they have done, or what it is they intend to do.

- Why did you do that?
- Why did you tell her that?
- Why are you going to run six more samples?

> People need to complain before they can create. This is important for managers to remember. Allow people to vent for a few minutes and then acknowledge what they're going through before moving them to a place of problem solving.

These types of questions put people in the defensive role, which usually shuts them down from further conversation. "Why" places you in the role of inquisitor and judge, not in the role of collaborator and coach. If possible, try to avoid the use of "why" when you coach. It is a very subtle difference, but can have a tremendous effect when you are trying to create a dialogue. Rephrase your "why" questions so that they encourage your employee to continue talking about the future (Table 3.5).

Table 3.5. *Rephrasing "Why" Questions*

"Why" Question	Possible Rephrasing
• Why did you do that? • Why did you tell her that? • Why are you going to run six more samples?	• What were you hoping to gain? • How did that work out for you? • How will running six more samples increase your confidence in the number?

Double whammy! Forward-focused why questions are almost always advice disguised as a question, so try your best to avoid them! "Why don't you just . . . ?" "Why not go to him and say . . . ?" "Why wouldn't you . . . ?" Our advice is, Why not just avoid them altogether?

THE W.I.N. B.I.G. COACHING FORMULA

Asking good questions is a necessity for a successful coaching conversation. However, asking someone a bunch of random questions does not necessarily mean that you are coaching them. As we said earlier in the chapter, a coaching conversation has three distinct components: 1) determining whether the situation requires coaching, 2) asking questions to create a dialogue that builds awareness about the issues at hand, and 3) moving the coachee to take action so that changes occur, leading to more effectiveness.

The Coaching Process

Determine Coachability ➡ Build Awareness ➡ Move to Action

There is a simple, six-step process you can follow to Build Awareness and Move to Action (Table 3.6). We call it the W.I.N. B.I.G. model because when you help an employee become aware of what's going on and then help them take action toward it, you WIN BIG and they WIN BIG. Coaching helps employees thrive in their jobs and increase their Level of Success in the Success Equation. When that happens, you have the time to focus on the work you do best, and you're empowering your team do the same. When this happens, it's a big win for everyone.

Table 3.6. *The Coaching Process*

Determine Coachability ⟹	Build Awareness ⟹	Move to Action
Is this about Aptitude, Attitude, or Available Resources?	W-onder about root cause I-nvestigate wants N-ame possible solutions	B-uild a plan I-nsure action G-ive affirmation

There are six steps in the W.I.N. B.I.G. model. Three of them Build Awareness and three Move to Action. They are:

Build Awareness

- W-onder about Root Cause—Discovery
- I-nvestigate Wants—Visioning
- N-ame Possible Solutions—Problem Solving

Move to Action

- B-uild a Plan—Action
- I-nsure Action—Accountability
- G-ive Affirmation—Validating

Creating a dialogue that progresses through these six steps will help you increase your employees' effectiveness, make you a better manager, and allow everyone involved to WIN BIG.

Build Awareness—W.I.N.

When there is a problem at hand, most people want to jump in and immediately move to action. It is often difficult to see the need, or benefit, of first taking a step back to build awareness about the situation and all that it entails. Whereas building awareness can help in any problem-solving scenario, it is vital when you are coaching to enhance an employee's Attitude. Therefore, be sure to start your coaching conversation by working through the three steps to Build Awareness. That's the only real way to WIN.

Build Awareness:

1. W-onder about root cause—Discovery
2. I-nvestigate wants—Visioning
3. N-ame possible solutions—Problem solving

W-onder about Root Cause—Discovery

It's easy to get caught up in a problem or crisis. It's easy to see that sales are decreasing, for instance, and assume that the sales team must be the problem. However, 99% of the time, what you see is just a symptom, not the real problem. You see the dying leaves of a tree, but not the dying roots. Fixing the dead leaves by spraying them with fungicide is only a band-aid; it may temporarily stop the leaves from dying but it's not going to fix the root cause. The same holds true when dealing with problems at work. Your job as a manager is to step back and contemplate the root cause of the problems that arise. Why are sales decreasing? What else is happening in the organization? How is your customer service? Quality of product? Competition? Delivery time? What are some other symptoms you see?

In the first step of coaching, Wonder about Root Cause, your job is to ask questions that will help your employee step back and look beneath the surface. Remember that they are human and will try to jump into problem solving, but just as firing the sales team probably won't help increase sales because it doesn't fix the real problem, you want to help the employee to identify the root cause to maximize their problem-solving efforts.

For a number of reasons, this stage can be a challenge for problem-solving managers. Notice the first word of this stage: Wonder. It's not Fix, Control, Stop, or any other action-hero type of word. It's Wonder. This word can be very hard for busy managers to accept. They often want to fix the problem and move on, essentially saying, "I'm not paid to wonder; I'm paid to know." But Wonder is the first step of successful coaching. Why? Because coaches don't, shouldn't, and can't have all the answers; the person in front of you has many more answers about themselves than you do. If you always fix the problem yourself, then you'll be known as a good fixer and a so-so manager at best. However, if you want to be known as a really good manager whose employees do great things for the organization, you need to empower them to do a better job by coaching them and helping them solve their own problems. You do that by helping them wonder and figure out how they are hindering themselves from being successful.

Start by getting curious. You know this employee can do good work, so what's going on? Is it a motivation problem? Don't judge it, just be curious about it. To the extent you can, be fascinated by how we humans all tick so differently from one another. You need to be curious, because you want your employee to be curious so they can Build Awareness. Take a deep breath and wonder. Ask curious questions in a manner that makes it fun, not scary. Think Discovery Channel. Have you ever watched their shows or played with their toys? They make discovery fun; they make it interesting, colorful, deep, and rich. They remind you of that cool teacher who made you curious about all kinds of things. That's what you're doing when you coach in this stage—you create a playful, contagious, curiosity about what's going on with the person in front of you so that they become curious too. You help them learn what the issue is, notice the feelings around the issue, and see the issues under the issue. Imagine peeling an onion—peel back the layers to get to what's really going on—all the while having fun and not judging the contents. Some good questions for this stage of the process are:

- How does that really affect you?
- If you were watching this on TV, what would you say was going on?
- What's the main obstacle getting in the way here?
- What's underneath all of this?
- Which of your buttons are really getting pushed here?

Don't confuse "Wonder about Root Cause" with getting all of the nitty-gritty details and facts about an issue. When Maria comes in frustrated about a conversation with Julie, you're not looking for the blow-by-blow details about who said what, or what time it took place. That will just get you into a no-win conversation. Instead, point out that she sounds angry and ask her what the anger's really about. You could ask her what's really frustrating her, what's the real issue, or what's the effect of Julie's recent conversation on her. As Maria opens up, you may realize, for example, that the real issue is that Julie is often late in getting her work to Maria who relies on it to meet her deadlines. So, the issue really isn't Maria's recent conversation with Julie. The issue is that Maria feels dumped on, overworked, unproductive, and underappreciated in her working relationship with Julie and these things are hindering Maria from being as effective and successful as she can be in her job. Had you not been curious and helped Maria wonder about the root cause of the

> When in this stage, remember to avoid "why" questions —you are not the judge; your job is to be a partner in Discovery.

> It is often asked, "Is it possible to wonder and navel gaze too much?" Use your judgment. When you have gotten to a place that seems like you are dealing with a real issue that directly affects Attitude, chances are it's time to move on.

problem, you would have focused on the original conversation she presented and probably left it at that. Because you helped build her awareness, however, you are now ready to coach her about how to have a more productive work environment and relationship with Julie—something that has a much bigger effect on the bottom line than discussing one isolated conversation.

So take the time to help your employee wonder and discover. Remember, you are building their awareness to increase effectiveness. Be curious and playful, and keep thinking Discovery Channel until you feel as though you have gathered enough information about the feelings and the root cause and then move on to stage two—Investigate Wants.

I-nvestigate Wants—Visioning

The more clear you are about what you want, the more likely you are to get it. Getting crystal clear on your wants greatly improves the results you get in life. We usually get what we say we want; the problem is, we usually aren't clear on what we *really* want so we end up with the wrong things. Lashon says she wants a new job. Eventually, she finds it but within a few months isn't happy—it's the same old stuff in a different place. Why? Because what she really wanted was more opportunity to be creative in a team environment with a more flexible schedule. If she had been clear about her wants before she started the job search, she would have been much more likely to find what she really wanted. This characteristic shows up in almost everything we do. Think about buying a house. How many times have you been in someone's relatively new home and heard the owner say, "Well, I wish we would have thought about . . ." or "If I was doing it again, I would look for . . ."? The more clear you are about what you want from a situation, the more likely you are to get it.

The goal of the second stage in W.I.N. B.I.G. is to help your employee investigate what it is that they really want (Investigate

Wants). In the first stage, you create safety by asking open-ended wonder-type questions and you get to the root cause of the problem. Next, it's time to look at what the person wants to have happen, how they want to be as things move forward, and what they want as the outcome. This requires you to ask questions that open up possibilities and help the person paint a clear picture of what they want. These questions help the employee think bigger and look to the future; here are some examples:

- What do you want?
- How would you like people to describe you as you resolve this?
- What would success look like?
- If you could use a magic wand to recreate the scene, how would you want it to look?

Again, it can be tempting here to jump into problem-solving mode. However, if you and your coachee begin creating solutions without clear knowledge of what the employee really wants, they might end up with something that still doesn't solve their situation

> Remember to keep your questions forward-focused, especially at this stage of the game. An employee's temptation will be to return to past events, but get them to look to the future. What do they really want the situation to look like and what kind of person do they want to be as they move forward?

in the most effective manner, just like Lashon and her new job. Additionally, it is important to spend a few minutes getting the person to focus on how they want "to be" as they go about doing what it is they want "to do." Help the person focus on what they really want from the situation and *who they want to be as they do it.* The latter is especially important because you are dealing with

Attitude—their motivation, determination, backbone, confidence, etc. For example, Abby can say she wants to resolve a situation, but does she want to do it in a way that is confident and self-assured or in a way in which she is a doormat to all the other players involved? Does she want to show up as an aggressive, cutthroat player or a collaborative partner in the process? Part of developing people is helping them grow into the vision of who it is that they want to be in their career and in life. This is the stage that lays the groundwork for that to happen. Without a clear vision of how they want to handle the situation at hand, they will probably problem-solve it using the same approaches they always have, getting the same results they've always gotten, and not developing at all.

It's important here more than anywhere else *not* to tell the employee what you think they should want. You have no way of knowing. We are all really good at thinking we know what others want, but we don't. Be sure to give the person space and time to figure it out for themselves. They may even need a few minutes of silence to think it through. Let them have that time without filling the empty space. Just sit back and know that they'll be able to do it. Your confidence in them will give them self-confidence. If they feel stuck, just ask another open-ended question about their desired outcome. The bottom line is: the employee knows. Deep down, we all know what we want. We just don't always get a chance to voice it. Now is the time to let your coachee voice it and be heard. They'll be much more involved in the action steps if you do. Often, when given the opportunity to be creative and "make it up," they discover their own right answer.

Suppose you have started talking to Jesse about his recent frustration over a team meeting. By Wondering about Root Cause, you've uncovered that his frustration isn't really about last week's meeting. It's about the fact that when he presents his ideas, he never feels like the team listens or seriously considers what it is he says, and as a result, he feels like he is viewed as an outsider who isn't con-

Because people can be so wrapped around the axle, they sometimes will say they don't know what they want. If you get an "I don't know" to one of your questions, respond by saying, "that's fine, make it up."

tributing to the bottom line. As you begin to Investigate Wants, you ask him, "How do you want to be viewed?"

Jesse: I want to be viewed as a leader on the team.

You: What would that look like? [You want him to get more clear on his wants.]

Jesse: I would have good ideas that the group would take and build on. People would look to me for answers and know that I was a reliable contributor to getting things done.

You: What else? [There is usually more; you can go until they say, "That's it."]

Jesse: I wouldn't have to bulldoze my ideas through; there wouldn't be the resistance from people that I am picking up now.

You: So, you want to be a knowledgeable leader on the team that people depend on for solutions. [This lets him know you heard and helps you confirm your understanding.]

Jesse: Exactly, and someone who helps other people get their ideas out there too.

As you can see, by asking three short, forward-focused questions, Jesse now has a much clearer picture of what it is he is trying to problem-solve toward. You started talking to him about his frustration over a meeting, and you are now talking with him about being a knowledgeable leader on the team whom people depend on for solutions. That's helping him cast a vision for how he wants to be on the team and in his career. Helping him get there will be a step in his development that he will value. But first, you have to help him figure out how to do it by moving to the step most people have been striving to get to, problem solving.

N-ame Possible Solutions—Problem Solving

There is a definite reason why this stage of W.I.N. is called Name Possible Solutions and not Name *the* Solution. Remember that you are still trying to Build Awareness, so the goal of this stage is to help the person become aware of the multitude of possible solutions and choices that they have in the situation as they move toward their vision. Typically, if left to our own devices, we humans will go about implementing the same solutions that have worked for us in the past—even if there is a potentially more effective or efficient way of going about it. As much as some of us don't like to admit it, we are creatures of habit. Our brains like to know how something is going to turn out, and we tend to stick to the tried and true. Think about the number of people who learn a route to work and stick to that route even if traffic gets backed up. Almost unconsciously, they will sit in traffic rather than venture off the route to find another way home. The same is true for us when we problem solve. That's why this stage is called, Name Possible Solutions, because in it your job is to get the employee to think big and outside the box, to explore all the possible options before settling on a specific strategy of action.

This is a tempting place for managers to jump in and solve the problem—to help the employee and maybe even save the day for them. But remember, coaching is about letting the person discover their own answers. It's not about you telling them what to do or you fixing it. You can, and should, help brainstorm during this problem-solving stage, but don't be attached to your ideas. Be prepared for, and OK with, the person rejecting your suggestions.

It can be difficult for some employees to reject an idea from their manager. If you think that might be the case, your statements could be qualified with prefaces such as, "This probably isn't it, but you could . . ." or "I'm not sure about this, but what if you. . . ." This will open the door for them to more comfortably push away your ideas.

Essentially, as a coach, you don't want the person to accept your idea—you want them to take it and build on it so that it becomes their own, more-improved version. Your goal is to help the employee open it up, have fun, and brainstorm. A good way to do that is to ask questions like:

- The 85-year-old you is looking back at this situation. What does she say to do?
- What are some ways to make that happen?
- What do you have to do to get where you want to go?
- How would Bill Gates tell you to solve the problem? Madonna?
- What would it take to work this out?

Asking follow-up questions is key. Do not settle with just one solution (even if you think it's a great one). Inspire your employee to think bigger and consider different options. So, ask follow-up questions or make statements like:

- What else?
- That's a great idea, what's another?
- Great, let's think of five more.

After you have generated many options, you need to start weighing the effects of the top ones. You'll want to help your coachee think through the possible solutions and play out what the effects would be on them, on the situation, and on all the stakeholders involved. One of the most important things you can do here is to help the person map back to what they said they wanted during Investigate Wants. Sure, their solution may solve the problem, but does it really get them what they want? When you have a few solutions on the table, ask questions like:

- So which option gets you closest to what you want?
- What would be the effects of your favorite solution?
- What possibility is your favorite? What would that get you?

Assume that Vernice is frustrated with her level of work. The amount that she has to do affects the quality of her projects as well as her life outside of work. As a result, she wants some work taken off her plate to bring more sanity, balance, and productiveness to her life. So, what are some possible ways to do that? In this phase, you Name Possibilities and brainstorm! Remember that in brainstorming you can be as wacky and wild as you want; it's about thinking outside of the box. There are no stupid, bad, or silly answers. So, Vernice could just go home at 5:00 p.m., no matter what. She could agree that the lowest-priority work won't get done. She could auction off some of work on eBay. She could hire someone. What about getting an intern/college student? Or hire her grandmother! She could alter the timeline of several projects. She could work from home two days a week. She could get better at saying no. Get the idea? There are hundreds of options here, so have fun and brainstorm with her. At the end, you could ask, "Which of the options gets you closest to what you want?"

Vernice: I'm really digging the idea of an intern.

You: What about that works for you? [You want to find out how that supports what she wants.]

Vernice: Well, I'd be able to get some of the more mundane tasks off my plate.

You: What else? [You want her to make as many connec-
          tions to her vision as possible.]

Vernice: I think it would be great to work with a student, to
          help teach them. It would be fun. I'd feel like I was
          giving back or something and it would make me
          aware of the quality of my work. . . .

By Naming Possible Solutions and opening Vernice to new
options, you have helped her to start devising a solution that not
only solves her problem, but also helps her develop in a way she
wants to grow—something that might not have happened had you
gone with the first solution she proposed. Creating the space and
fun to think big is vital in this stage. Of course, it means nothing if
you don't make a plan and Move to Action, which is where you take
the employee next (see Table 3.6, p. 59).

It is possible that the employee will come up with a solution with
which you disagree or can't support because of the business
repercussions. If that's the case, say something like, "That's a
possible solution; here's what I can get behind and here's what
part (and why) I can't support. What else could get you where
you want to go that takes those concerns into account?"

Move to Action—B.I.G.

After you have helped someone Build Awareness, they are in a great
position to not only implement a winning course of action, but to
also have the commitment they will need to follow through with the
plan. Action is the key here. Remember that you can Build
Awareness all day long, but if you never Move to Action, you have
done nothing but have nice conversations with your employee. The
goal is concrete action—doing things differently to reach higher lev-

els of success. There are three steps to follow as you move someone to succeed in a BIG way.

Move to Action:

1. B-uild a plan—Action
2. I-nsure action—Accountability
3. G-ive affirmation—Validation

B-uild a Plan—Action

People love this stage. Now you can start moving and grooving. You can finally Build a Plan that gets you to some action. But again, most of this decision will come from the coachee, not you. What is it going to take for them to implement the solution that they have chosen? What are the tangible steps that they will take so that things look differently in the future? Your goal in this stage is to help the employee devise a realistic plan that gets them where they want to go in a doable manner and timeframe.

This is the stage at which you get down to the details. Vague and abstract ideas don't work here. You are going for specific action steps that move the employee towards their solution. To Build a Plan, you'll want to ask questions like:

- What are you going to do?
- What steps do you have to take to get there?
- When will you do that?
- Who do you need to bring into the process?
- What will you have to say no to in order to make this happen?

As a coach, it's OK to challenge your employees during this stage. The reason you're coaching them is because of the hurdles that are preventing them from growing. Overcoming or dismantling these

You'll notice here that your questions begin to get more specific and, to a certain degree, more closed-ended. It is fine to ask, "Will you do that by next Friday?" The answer will probably be yes or no, and that's fine in this stage because you need specifics.

hurdles can be a tremendous challenge that is usually approached with some degree of trepidation. For that reason, watch and listen to your coachee. Do you get the sense they are not believing in themselves enough or holding back somewhat? If so, challenge them by upping the ante of their actions. Throw your suggestion out there and see what they say. If they say yes, great. If they say no, ask them if they have a counteroffer. Usually, they will respond with an action that is somewhat more aggressive than the one they had initially proposed. See Table 3.7 for some ideas about how to challenge an employee as they Build a Plan.

As your employee is creating their plan, help them to make it SMART: Specific, Measurable, Achievable, Realistic, and Time-specific. As we've pointed out above, the person's actions should be very specific; this is no time for vagueness. Also, find a way to make things measurable, even if they are measured by "yes, I did it" or "no, I didn't do it." The action steps also need to be achievable so the employee can see their progress and feel good about it. Goals and tasks often need to be chunked down to manageable pieces; otherwise, the person gets overwhelmed and gives up. So, if necessary, break the actions into achievable pieces so they can do a little every week and be able to report on progress. The action steps also need to be realistic considering the employee's circumstances. Having someone say they are going to increase annual sales by 80% in a week is probably a bit of a stretch. Finally, be sure to have a timeline in place. The purpose of coaching is to stretch and develop your employees. Most people need some time pressure to make that hap-

Table 3.7. *Challenging an Employee to Build a Plan*

Employee Response	A Potential Challenge
• To make it happen, I'd have to make five sales calls a week for a month . . .	• Great. Could you make nine calls a week?
• OK, I'll sit down and have a conversation with her by next Friday . . .	• Hm . . . how about this Friday?
• Well, I could announce the idea at next month's staff meeting . . .	• You "could," or you "will"? How about sending out an e-mail this week?

pen. If you and your coachee are SMART, then success will come more easily because there was a plan from the beginning.

A quick side note about action and building a plan. Sometimes, continuing to Build Awareness is a great action. For example, Marcos comes to you to talk about how he can never get what he needs out of the finance group. Through your coaching, Marcos realizes that perhaps his agitation seeps through in his conversation with the people in finance and affects the way he makes his requests. As an action, he decides to spend a week or so paying attention to his conversations to look for ways that his frustration might be leaking out. He also wants to pay attention to how clearly he makes his requests during that time period. Both of these "actions" are good ones for coaching. Before Marcos can really Build a Plan, he may need more information about his own actions and how he's affecting other people. That's fine, as long as you loop back in a week or so and take the coaching further. Not every coaching conversation has to end with a change-the-world type of plan; sometimes committing to observation for the sake of self-awareness can be a huge action step.

Regardless of the chosen solution, your job here is to help Build a Plan. Be specific and don't be afraid to throw out a challenge or two. In the long run, your employee will thank you for pushing them to success. Everyone needs a little help when setting new goals, which is the very reason that you spend time in the next stage of the process—to Insure Action.

I-nsure Action—Accountability

One of the most important things a manager can do as a coach is hold the person accountable for the actions to which they've committed. As the person leaves the coaching conversation and gets sucked back into the black hole that is their busy life, it is natural for the insights they gained to become blurred and for their planned actions to become a bit more daunting. Left to their own devices, most people will let things slip back to status quo and then fall back into their old routines. That's what makes this stage of the coaching process so important. Your goal here is to Insure Action by establishing an accountability system. Having the coachee say they are going to do something is not enough. Here, you want to ask specific questions like:

- How will I know?
- When will you let me know how it goes?
- How much time do you need before checking back in with me?
- How will I know if you need a nudge?
- What's the best way for you to circle back to me?

It can be great to follow up these questions with a conversation about what you should do if the person doesn't follow through on their commitments. Questions like these are good ways to start off the conversation:

- What should I do if you don't get back to me?
- How would you like me to follow up if I don't hear back?

- If you don't follow through, how should I help get you back into gear?

Some people prefer an e-mail reminder, some want a personal visit because they respond well to pressure. Talk about what will work for the person, and then make sure that if need be, you do it! The key here is to do it compassionately and frankly: "Hi Felicia. . . . My calendar says you were supposed to have a conversation with Maurice by today. How did it go?" You don't need to cajole, threaten, or beg. She made the commitment; you're just checking in.

Many managers say at this point, "Why should I have to worry about them following through? If they really want to make the changes or right the problem, then they will do it. If they don't, it's their loss." That's understandable. And, it's important to be realistic.

Insuring Action puts some responsibility back on you. It's the part of the coaching process in which you have an action item. You will have to do whatever it takes to keep your end of the bargain. Be sure that what you commit to is realistic given your schedule. Not following up can send a bad signal to the employee and set you up for future problems.

How many times have you said you were going to stop procrastinating your expense reports until the last minute, or you were going to do a better job at standing up to your boss? We all have things we'd like to do to become more effective. We all have good intentions. When we have a problem with our Attitude, it is difficult to fix by ourself, and often we need a little help. The assistance you provide to your employees in this area by setting up an accountability structure is key to their continued development, and their continued development is part of your managerial responsibility and crucial to your overall success.

The whole goal of accountability is that eventually the employee becomes accountable to themselves, not you. You will not always be available to coach them. However, as they learn these new skills and practice them over time with you, they will eventually learn how to hold themselves accountable. This is called empowerment. They'll feel empowered to try new things on their own because of the skills they learned with you.

Another note about accountability is that it is often a dance that leads to more coaching. Sometimes the person does everything

Follow Up to Insure Action

The "action" of a coaching conversation does not happen during the conversation; it begins when the conversation ends and the coachee sets out to do something differently than before. To ensure that the action moves forward, it is important to set up an accountability structure with your coachee. Even more important is for you to follow through on your follow up! Depending on the situation, after a few days or weeks, be sure to check in to see how the person is doing on their commitments. Here are a few example questions you can use to get the ball rolling as you follow up.

- How is it working? How is it going?
- How would you summarize the work/effort so far?
- What's working well? What are you thinking of altering?
- What's the learning in this situation?
- What have you learned about yourself?
- If you were to do this again, what would you do differently?
- What was the lesson for you in all of this?
- What will you take away from this?
- How will you lock in and solidify the learning?
- What can I do to be supportive as you move forward?

they committed to do exactly as planned, sometimes they drag their feet and do it late, and sometimes they don't do it all. If your employee dragged their feet or didn't do what they said they wanted to do, you may need to sit down and go back to the Wonder-about-Root-Cause step to find out what happened. What stopped them? What got in the way of the follow through? How do they explain missing the deadline to themselves? Do they believe their excuse? What are the feelings around that? It's natural as a coaching manager to feel frustrated if this happens. Do your best to stay curious about why the employee is still in their own way. Do your best to want the best for them and to see them succeed. Do your best not to judge their efforts and instead, try to feel compassion. But also do your best to push them to define a new action to which you can hold them accountable again.

G-ive Affirmation—Validation

The final stage of the coaching process is one that can be used anywhere during the coaching conversation, but especially at the end. This is a very important step and one that most people forget. What your employee has committed to accomplish may be easy for you, but could be a challenge for them; otherwise, they wouldn't be asking for your help. So take the time to Give Affirmation and acknowledge their hard work and their desire to grow and change. Your purpose here is to validate the goals, efforts, and plans that the person is putting forth and to validate the strengths or qualities that you see, think, or know will make them successful as they move forward. This is a time for you to encourage, inspire, and motivate by saying things like:

- I just want to take a second and point out how much progress you've made in the past three weeks. You're really smart and your plan is perfect. Look how far you've come!

- You know, you're really stepping up to the plate. It takes a lot of courage to look at yourself and see how you can be more effective. It's a sign of a real leader.
- I have no doubt you can do this. You're determined and persistent. I know there's a lot to this, but your energy is contagious and others are going to get on board.

That being said, validating statements look different to everyone, and sound differently coming from different people. A lot of managers get nervous in this stage, wondering what it is that they are supposed to say. You just say what you know is true about that person. It doesn't have to be overly sentimental. Make sure it rolls easily off your tongue, which will happen if it's sincere. It can be as simple as saying, "Your ability to listen to others helps them trust you." Or, "It takes strength and courage to change the status quo. You've got both of those qualities in large amounts." Or, "When you speak, people listen to you and want to follow you." Just let the person know that you see what they're trying to do, you see their special qualities, and you will support them in any way you can. It's that simple.

As we pointed out above, you do not have to wait until the end of the conversation to Give Affirmation. You can do it at any point during the process. You can interrupt the conversation at any time by saying something like, "I just want to jump in for a second and point out that this is the most energy I've seen you have about this project in a long time; you seem excited." Or, "before we move on, I want to let you know that I know this has been holding you back for a long time. Congrats on grabbing it by the horns. . . ." These interruptions will inject energy into your conversation and help the employee think bigger and plan more aggressively. They want, and need, to know that you believe in their ability to make the change they committed to. They need to hear you say that you know they can do it, because chances are they are doubting themselves on some level—or else they would have done it already. So get in the habit of giving affirmation at various points, not only throughout your coaching conversations but in *any* conversation you are having with your employees.

When you Give Affirmation, be prepared to follow it with a brief pause. People are not used to hearing good things about themselves, and for many people, receiving validation is actually an uncomfortable experience. When you are in this stage, or anytime that you are pointing out someone's strengths, take a few seconds at the end of your statement and "let it land." This means that before you move on to the next thing, pause for a second or two so that the employee has a better chance of letting your comment register and stick.

Putting It All Together to W.I.N. B.I.G.

You are now set to WIN BIG! Using this formula will not only help you succeed, but more importantly, it will help you to help others succeed. Once you have determined the coachability of a situation, focus on asking questions that create a dialogue that builds awareness and then move the person to action. To do that, use the W.I.N. B.I.G. model to help you wonder about root cause, investigate wants, and name the possibilities. When you have narrowed down your possible solutions, build a plan, insure action, and give affirmation to the employee as they set out to be more successful.

COACHING FREQUENTLY ASKED QUESTIONS

The truth is, we know that coaching can be a little overwhelming at first. So we've designed this book to help you with the process. The final chapters of this book contain nothing but questions for you to use in each stage of the coaching process. You can use them as a resource and guide as you work your way through coaching conversations. Chapter 5 explains in detail how to make the best use of those chapters. But, for now, let's look at a few frequently asked questions managers often have about coaching.

1. **How long should I spend in each phase?**

    It will be different in each situation. Sometimes one or two questions are enough if they are focused and get to the point. A coaching conversation can take just a few minutes or it can take an hour. The key is to proceed slowly and take the time you need. No matter how long it takes, coaching should never feel rushed. See Chapter 5 for how to use this book to help employees when you're not available or don't have time for a coaching conversation.

2. **Is W.I.N. B.I.G. a linear process?**

    Not necessarily. Be prepared to backtrack sometimes. You may be in the middle of Naming Possibilities and realize that there is really something deeper going on, so slip back to Wondering about Root Cause. The only linear aspect about coaching is that you should always Build Awareness before you Move to Action.

3. **What do I do if things get too emotional?**

    This is different for everyone, depending on your comfort level. Remember that as much as we may want it to happen, people cannot "check their emotions at the door." It's just not possible. During a coaching conversation, people may get angry, sad, or happy—the key is to let them feel their emotion. Chances are, they will *not* get too emotional. We've been coaching for years and can count the number of times things have gotten "too emotional" on one hand (between us!). "Coaching could get emotional" is typically an unrealistic fear that keeps managers from trying to coach. If, for some reason, you start to feel uncomfortable, take a few deep breaths and remind yourself that the person is completely capable of taking care of themselves. You don't have to fix anything, including their emotions. Then, check in with the person. How are they doing? Do they want to take a break? Is the coaching process helping? Continue to stay calm and let the employee decide what to do.

4. **This is too much to remember. What if I mess it up?**

If your intent is to create a dialogue that leads an employee to higher levels of effectiveness, then you can't mess up. The intent is really what counts in the whole coaching process. Build awareness through curiosity. Once you both have an understanding, move to action by asking, "So what are you going to do about this?" If your intent is to see them succeed, you'll be great. The W.I.N. B.I.G. stuff is all finesse, so don't sweat it.

5. **How do I know if this is working?**

If you try to coach during the appropriate times, you will see people change. That's how you know. Keep your eyes open and watch them. Get excited about their growth. Ask them how they are doing. Look for the small steps as well as the big ones. Give Affirmation and Insure Action by holding people accountable. You'll see, and then you'll know.

6. **Does this work outside of work?**

Coaching is not just a work skill, it's a great life skill. Using this type of conversation—one in which you listen with the intent of helping the other person overcome their own hurdles—works wonders anywhere.

7. **What if I forget the process in the middle of a conversation?**

Until you get the hang of it, use this book as a resource. Keep it out and use the chapters in the back during your coaching meetings. If all else fails, go back to the basics: 1. Build Awareness—what's really going on here? and 2. Move to Action—so, what are you going to do about it?

8. **What if I disagree with or think that the solution my employee develops is a bad idea?**

It is quite possible that while helping your employee develop a solution they will want to pursue an idea with which you disagree or cannot support. If this happens, first ask yourself whether you disagree because the solution is against company policy or will not yield the end results that you need, or if you disagree simply because the employee's way is not your way of tackling the problem. As a manager, you have the right to step in and reverse an employee's decision, but if you disagree simply because their way is not your way, then we strongly advise against it because this could have serious long-term consequences. If you are really trying to develop this employee and they devise a solution that is different than your approach, but has a decent chance of yielding the results you need, you should consider stepping back and letting them try. If, however, you are fairly certain the employee's solution will not succeed, a good approach is to use what we call the ALT-Alt flow of conversation (Affirm, Like, Trouble, Alternatives). In this model, you *Affirm* the employee's thinking, state what you *Like* about the proposed solution, explain what *Troubles* you about the solution, and then brainstorm *Alternatives* that address your concern. It goes something like this:

You:	The logic and thinking behind your solution are sound and it makes sense to me how you came up with it (*Affirm*). Do you mind if I weigh in on the situation?
Employee:	Sure, go ahead.
You:	What I like about your idea is that it covers all of the bases in an innovative way and it would bring the project in under budget with time to spare (*Like*). I'd like to figure out how to keep that part of the plan.
Employee:	Great . . . and?
You:	And, what concerns me about the solution is that it has the potential of alienating our biggest client, which could have some serious effects (*Trouble*).

Can we brainstorm some ways that would include them in the process in a more active way (*Alternatives*)?

You don't have to like the ideas your employees come up with, but you do have to tell them in a way that empowers them and keeps them returning to be coached.

9. **Can you use coaching to make a good situation even better?**
Yes! Remember that a really high Attitude can sometimes help people achieve a high Level of Success despite the fact that they have a lower Aptitude or a lack of Available Resources. For that reason, it can be a great idea to coach employees who already have a good Attitude about a certain task in order to help them have even higher Levels of Success. Granted, we have focused much of this book on how to use coaching to enhance an employee's Attitude when there is an issue or problem with the task they are performing. This is because, in our experience, managers experience the most frustration with employees whose Attitude is less than optimal. For that reason, we have intentionally focused primarily on times when an employee's Attitude stands in the way of their success. However, coaching also works to make great employees even better. In those situations, when you Wonder about Root Cause, frame the conversation something like this:

You: You are doing a really great job as a project lead for the Allin project.
Employee: Thanks, I appreciate it.
You: On a scale of 1 to 10, how would you rate your performance?
Employee: I think I'd give myself an 8.
You: What would you be doing differently to give yourself a 9? What's standing in your way of clicking it up a notch?

Use a conversation like the one above to start the process of Wondering how an employee could "turn it up" a little. If you discover that they are creating barriers for improvement, then coach them using the W.I.N. B.I.G. model. If you find they lack Aptitude or Available Resources, take the appropriate actions discussed earlier in the chapter. Either way, coaching is not just about dealing with employee-problem issues. It is also a great way to make high performance even higher.

10. **What if I can't think of a question to ask?**

First, you can consult Chapters 6 and 7 of this book, which are filled with a variety of questions. But if you are stuck, you can say something like, "I'm not sure what question I should ask you next. If you were me, what would you ask?" You'll be surprised at the questions (and answers) they present.

Once you know the W.I.N. B.I.G. model, you can coach in any situation. In fact, the W.I.N. B.I.G. model is somewhat like a game. It can be fun, the rules are straightforward, you know what to do next, and you get to play and be creative in the different stages. So no matter what you do when coaching, try to think of it as a game and keep it light and easy. It takes time and practice. But it's well worth it when your coachee hits a home run and moves forward in life!

4

The Tenets of Coaching

If you read coaching books and take coaching courses, you'll notice that everyone has a slightly different definition of coaching. In addition, everyone (including professionals) puts their own spin on their coaching, no matter where they learned to coach. Coaching styles can be compared to the stripes on a zebra. Just as no two zebras have the same stripes, no two people will have the same style of talking, writing, and being. Each coach brings their unique qualities to a coaching conversation, creating their own style. In addition, coaching is a fluid process. It is a dance of give and take between the coach and the coachee in which no two conversations are ever alike. Naturally, then, everyone is going to coach a bit differently based on their unique training, style, and situation.

There may not be one right way to coach, but there are some basic tenets that are common to coaches, regardless of what model they learned or what style they use. We have broken these tenets into three groups (Table 4.1): Coaching Mindset, Coaching Actions, and Coaching Tricks of the Trade. Many would argue that the majority of these tenets apply to more than just coaching, and if integrated

Table 4.1. *The Coaching 21*

Coaching Mindset

1. **Believe in Potential**
   The coach fully believes that the coachee has the potential to handle the situation at hand in a way that is more productive, less stressful, or more efficient than is currently happening.

2. **Be Unattached**
   The coach truly believes that the coachee will find the best solution to their own problem, and the coach is consequently willing to set aside their own solutions to the coachee's problem.

3. **Don't Know and Don't Fix It**
   The coach lets go of the need to know the answers or provide a solution and consequently helps the coachee believe that they know everything they need to know to find the best solution.

4. **Keep It Light and Fun!**
   Coaching shouldn't be heavy. Creativity is a great tool for solving problems and adults learn best when they're having fun and being interactive. Need we say more?

5. **Stay Curious**
   The coach remains curious and unattached to the coachee's answers, listening without judgment, asking questions, and not giving answers or telling the coachee how to fix the problem.

6. **Trust Your Gut**
   The coach listens to and acts upon their gut reactions, allowing the coachee to examine his own gut instincts and move to a different level of problem solving.

7. **Build Awareness Before Action**
   Without a good process, accomplishing the task at hand is difficult. Coaches work to build awareness before they move to action.

Coaching Actions

8. **Mirror**
   The coach holds up a "mirror" to the coachee, explaining to the coachee what the coach sees in the situation at hand. The coach lets the coachee interpret the data.

9. **Listen**
   The coach focuses 100% on the coachee's words, emotions, and body language in order to gain a deeper understanding and ask the next question based on what the coachee said.

10. **Create Space**
    The coach prepares for a coaching session, and not only clears the area of all physical distractions (e-mail, crackberry, etc), but clears themselves mentally as well.

11. **Validate**

   The coach acknowledges what the coachee is going through and/or what they have accomplished, and then points out something that the coachee may not see in themselves regarding how they have dealt with the situation.

12. **Ask**

   The coach asks open-ended questions that will empower the coachee to find their own answers for the problem at hand, as well as future problems.

13. **Feedback**

   The coach gives specific feedback regarding one or more of the coachee's behaviors, and the effect of those behaviors. This is typically followed by asking the coachee to create an alternative behavior that will lead to an alternative effect.

14. **Celebrate**

   The coach acknowledges what the coachee has accomplished and helps them find a way to mark the achievement.

Coaching Tricks of the Trade

15. **Bottom Line**

   The coachee or coach summarizes the situation at hand in a few words or 2–3 sentences to reach appropriate conclusions.

16. **Word Choice**

   The coach is consciously aware of the words they use in a coaching session, and listens for, and points out, "red flag" words that a coachee uses that may prevent them from moving forward.

17. **Story Shift**

   The coach reminds the coachee that there are many stories, or perspectives, about the problem at hand and encourages them to look at the problem in a different perspective.

18. **Coach the Person**

   The coach keeps the focus on the coachee, and not someone else in the coachee's situation because you can't change other people, only the coachee's reaction to them.

19. **Deal with Resistance**

   The coach continues to ask questions in a detached manner even when a coachee refuses to look at an issue in any other way than their own, or feels that they do not need coaching on an issue.

20. **Address Fears**

   The coach helps the coachee identify and confront fears that stop them from moving forward.

21. **Create Vision**

   The coach helps the coachee determine their vision of where they want to be in 2–5 years, as a way to help the coachee successfully grow and develop in the right direction.

into a manager's daily interaction with employees, would greatly enhance one's overall effectiveness. Although it may feel daunting to read all 21 tenets, we suggest that you take the time to look through them. You don't have to memorize them all, but understanding these tenets will help you become a better coach and ultimately a better manager. Let's take a look at the three groupings and then we'll break each down in greater detail.

COACHING MINDSET

The first seven tenets are the lens you look through when coaching. They will help you approach a coaching conversation with an open mind, allowing both you and the coachee the necessary space to create an effective coaching conversation. If these tenets are not followed, a coaching conversation could become a dead-end conversation because the necessary coaching attitude and mindset aren't in place. The components of the Coaching Mindset are:

- Believe in Potential
- Be Unattached
- Don't Know and Don't Fix It
- Keep It Light and Fun
- Stay Curious
- Trust Your Gut
- Build Awareness Before Action

COACHING ACTIONS

Having the right lens for approaching coaching is not enough. There are some specific things you need to do and some different skills you need to apply during a coaching conversation. These tenets are the practical aspects of coaching. We recommend that you use these skills on a regular basis in almost every coaching conversation. They can (and should) be easily incorporated into the W.I.N. B.I.G. model (Chapter 3). As you gain more confidence in coaching, using these tenets will come naturally to you, allowing you to become a stronger coach. These Coaching Actions are:

- Mirror
- Listen
- Create Space
- Validate
- Ask
- Feedback
- Celebrate

COACHING TRICKS OF THE TRADE

These tenets are several of the tricks of the trade that coaches pick up over the years. You won't need to use these tenets in each coaching conversation. However, you may need to keep them in mind so that when the occasion arises, you can use them appropriately. They'll help you be more effective and in some cases help your coaching go more smoothly. The seven tricks we've included are:

- Bottom Line
- Word Choice
- Story Shift
- Coach the Person
- Deal with Resistance
- Address Fears
- Create Vision

Again, don't worry about remembering all these tenets at once. Use this book as a reference when needed. We recommend that you practice one tenet at a time, until you feel you have mastered it. Then choose another tenet until you feel you have mastered that one. Eventually, these will all feel like natural tools to use not only in coaching, but also in your day-to-day managerial tasks as well. Now that's what we call a win-win!

The following pages break each of the 21 tenets down with more explanation and further examples.

THE SEVEN TENETS OF COACHING MINDSET

Believe in Potential

In order to coach someone, the coach has to believe that the coachee has the potential to handle the situation at hand in a way that is more productive, less stressful, or more efficient than is currently happening. We often work with managers who talk about how good a certain employee or team is during a specific situation. They say things like:

- Oh, but when the pressure is on, she can really kick it into high gear.
- The team clicks like clockwork when there is a crisis at hand.
- He is at his best when he's focused on landing a major deal.

As a manager, you have seen your employees thrive during certain times and situations—you have seen them excel, and more than likely, you have benefited as a result. What if your employees were "at their best," "clicking like clockwork," and "kicked into high gear," more of the time? When you coach an employee, you have to believe that they have the potential to be *that good* in every situation.

Be Unattached

This is perhaps the hardest coaching skill for managers to learn. As we've pointed out before, the best way for people to become aware of what's going on is for *them* to discover it and to figure out what

TIP   Believe in Potential

We all get into situations in which we have difficulty believing in someone's potential. Things happen, our vision gets clouded, they get on our nerves, and we forget that people really are capable of achieving great results. The truth is, everyone has potential to achieve great things and perform at a higher level. If you need some help getting your mindset back on track, spend a few minutes thinking about your employee and work through the following questions:

- When is the person at their best? It may even be a situation you have heard about outside of work.
- When have you caught a glimpse of what they are capable of?
- Jot down some of the characteristics and traits that you saw in the person at that time (i.e., focused, productive, charismatic, and funny).
- Now ask yourself, "If the person has the ability to be focused, productive, charismatic, and funny during that time, what is it that keeps me from seeing them this way more of the time?" and "What would be the impact if they were like that more of the time?"

You have seen them be that way—they *can* be that way more often. As a coach, you have to believe it, even if they don't.

they should do about it. Because of this, as a coaching manager, you have to be prepared to play the role of creating a dialogue that leads to awareness and action. This doesn't mean that you won't have valuable opinions, thoughts, and ideas. What it does mean is that if you are *really* coaching, you can't be attached to them. That means you have to be OK with the employee rejecting your ideas, or building on them. You have to be prepared to throw ideas out there and have the employee say, "No, I don't think that's it," and then continue the conversation. The reason this is so hard for managers is because managers are good at devising solutions and giving orders that "fix it." Remember, if a person needs coaching, they don't need you to fix it for them; they need you to help them step back and get out of the weeds so that they can make solid decisions from a place of effectiveness and empowerment instead of a place where they are wrapped around the axle. The way to do that is to be unattached to your ideas and suggestions.

TIP   Be Unattached

The best way to stay unattached is to believe that the employee will find the best solution themselves. You must also believe that if you throw out a suggestion that doesn't work for an employee, it will lead them to something that does. Here are some good follow-up questions for when a coachee doesn't go for an idea, thought, or suggestion you present to them.

Possible Employee Response	Typical Manager's Response	Better Coaching Question
• No, I don't think that's it . . .	• Well, why not?	• Great, what *do* you think it is?
• I'm not sure that'd work . . .	• I think it would, if you'd try it.	• OK, what *would* work?
• I don't think I could do *that* . . .	• Sure you could.	• Well, what *could* you do?

There may be times when you disagree with, or cannot support, an employee's idea when you are coaching them. See item 8 under *Coaching Frequently Asked Questions* in Chapter 3 for ideas about how to deal with that situation.

Coaching is needed when employees have the skills but something else is going on. If you are attached to your recommendation of a specific way the employee should handle a situation, it may be an indicator that coaching is not the right tool for the situation. If that's the case, teach, don't coach. (See When to Coach and When Not to Coach in Chapter 2.)

Don't Know and Don't Fix It

Good managers delegate well, communicate well, and see the bigger picture at work. They don't necessarily know the minute details of each of their employees' projects, and that's a good thing. It's not their job to know every element of every project. That's the employee's job; a manager's job is to know the bigger picture and orchestrate all the projects so that together they work like a well-oiled machine. Yes, managers need to understand the basics of projects so that they can help employees move in the right direction, but being concerned with all the fine print bogs managers down and keeps them from doing their job effectively.

The same goes for coaching. You don't need to know every detail of every topic in order to coach someone. In fact, you don't even need to know *anything* about their issue to coach them. In theory this sounds easy, but it's not for most managers. Managers are good at fixing things, so they may fall into the trap of asking about the details so that they can find the answers for the coachee. That's not your job as a coach. Your job is to help the coachee see the bigger picture of their issue, and help them believe that they know everything they need to know to find the solution they're looking for. Your job is to ask questions that prompt them to do their best thinking. Then sit back and let them find their own solution. You will do your best coaching when you don't know the answers and don't try to fix it!

TIP   Don't Know and Don't Fix It

When you coach someone, it's OK (and even encouraged!) to say that you don't know the answer and trust that they *do* know the answer, even if they don't think they do. This not only empowers them, enabling them to grow and develop, but it also allows you to move forward in your own work, rather than delving into the minutia of theirs.

Here are some good follow-up questions if a coachee asks for help. Remember, you might have an answer, but if this is really a situation that calls for coaching, you want the coachee to come up with a solution on their own.

Possible Employee Response	Typical Manager's Response	Better Coaching Question
I don't know how to fix this problem.	Well, here's what you do . . .	What's the biggest thing standing in the way?
I've tried every-thing; nothing is working.	So, what have you tried?	OK, take a step back. What haven't you tried/done yet that you know you really ought to try/do?
I think we need to start from scratch.	That's not possible, we'll have to make this work.	Great. What would that look like and how would it affect the project timeline?

Keep It Light and Fun!

Managing people at work can be tough. People are human and, like it or not, they bring their emotions, issues, and perspectives to work with them: Judith is angry about something the marketing group did, Sonya is going through a divorce, and Tom is dealing with aging parents. Not to mention the multitude of other emotion-provoking

---

TIP   Keep It Light and Fun!

People learn best when they're having fun and interacting. So it's OK to show your silly side; it helps your coachee lighten up too. Appropriate jokes, songs, games, and physical movements all add to coaching in ways that sitting at a desk can't. However, it's important to ensure that the silliness is appropriate and that good follow-up questions are asked on the other side. Here are some tips for making coaching more fun and creative:

Possible Employee Response	*Possible Follow-Up Responses*
I'm feeling stuck right now.	I'm feeling stuck too. Let's take a walk around the block and see if we come up with anything new.
I don't know what the next step is.	Me either. Let's play a game. Starting with "A," let's name possible things you could do for each letter of the alphabet, no matter how silly it sounds. I'll go first and we'll alternate ideas. " 'A' . . . you could Ask the client to change the parameters; your turn, 'B.' "
	It's like there is a mountain of obstacles to climb. We need Diana Ross—what's that song she sings? What do you think she'd tell you to do in this situation?

scenarios—deadlines, staff cuts, lack of resources, and the new competition. Sometimes having a coaching conversation with Sonya is the last thing you want to do in a hectic day. It simply feels difficult and like one more thing on your to-do list.

We get it. *And* we know that coaching doesn't have to be dreary and hard. In fact, coaching can actually be quite fun! Creativity is a great tool for finding a solution to a problem, but it's hard to be creative in an atmosphere of seriousness and hard work. Fun and humor are great ways to access creativity, allowing the right side of your brain to find a solution you might not have thought of if you were too serious. So although coaching is a serious management tool, that doesn't mean you have to always be serious when coaching. In fact, some of the best coaching we've seen is when people have been at their silliest and wildest! So clear off your desk and have some fun with it! If you do, both you and your employee will feel better just from having a few laughs!

Stay Curious

Curiosity is underrated in the workplace. As children, we're encouraged to be curious, to explore, and to learn by asking questions. But as we take exams, apply for jobs, and become managers, we're expected to know everything, which can be exhausting. As a coach, you're not expected to know everything. The more curious you are, the more space you give the employee to explore and find the answers they need. So, when listening to an employee, keep your "problem-solving-fix-it train" from leaving the station too soon. Stay focused on what the employee is saying, and ask yourself, "I wonder what this is all about?"

Your job is to believe in the person's potential and be curious about how they are blocking their own success. Ask simple, curious questions that help the coachee discover their own answer. When this happens, the employee is empowered to find more solutions on

TIP   Stay Curious

Your job as a coach is to be curious, and to be unattached to the coachee's answer. Avoid judging an answer, giving advice, or telling them how to fix a problem. By remaining curious, your coachee is given space to be curious too, which aids in finding new solutions to their own problem. You're also modeling for them how to be curious, so that, on their own, they may find solutions to future problems. Here are some good questions to ask that help you and your coachee remain curious about the solutions to a problem:

Possible Employee Response	Typical Manager's Response	Better Coaching Question
I missed my sales targets again. I need help.	Yeah, I've been thinking of ways to deal with that . . .	Yeah . . . so what are the things that are getting in your way?
This project is much more complicated and difficult than I expected.	Well let me break it down for you . . .	What has you hung up the most?
I don't know . . . she's just driving me up a wall!	Well, let me tell you about how I deal with her . . .	Sounds like she is stepping on something you value, like your commitment to quality, perhaps. What is it?

their own and therefore develop in their job, rather than just taking orders from you without giving any input to the solution. Curiosity also keeps the fun factor alive, while allowing you to stay unattached to the reply. Although it can feel odd at first, coaching from a place of curiosity can actually be a fun relief because you don't have to know the answer and can just sit back and be child-like and curious for a few moments during the day.

Trust Your Gut

Trusting your gut instinct is vital to becoming a successful manager. Trusting your instincts can show up in different ways; it could be a funny feeling in your stomach, an adrenaline rush, tingly fingers, headache, or nagging doubts. The best managers use their instincts to guide their actions. If something doesn't feel right to them, even if it looks good on paper, they investigate it further to see if anything is missing or miscalculated, or they might bag it all together. If something *does* feel right, even if all the numbers don't quite add up, they usually analyze it one more time before going ahead and taking a chance on it.

The same is true for coaching. Trust your instincts when coaching someone. If you're talking about a problem and you get a nagging doubt, adrenaline rush, or funny feeling in your stomach, trust that sensation and use it in the conversation. You don't know what the coachee will say in response, and you're not interpreting the instinct and telling them what to do. You're just telling them what your instincts are telling you and they can then use that information as they create the solution to their own problem. Learning to trust your instincts can take time; it's like a muscle that needs to be used on a regular basis. However, using it regularly will not only help you find your own solutions to problems, but it will also model this skill to your coachee, helping them strengthen it over time for their own growth and development.

TIP   Trust Your Gut

When you coach someone, it's OK to bring your instincts into the conversation. The key is not to get attached to the outcome. You may get a nagging doubt but the coachee may get a tingly feeling. Your job is not to tell them to trust *your* instincts and insist that your instincts are right; your job is to put it on the table and let them tell you what they think. They may completely disagree with what you said, but by accessing your instincts, you're helping them access and trust their own instincts. They may say, "No, my stomach doesn't feel queasy. But my heart is pumping fast. When that happens, usually it means that I'm on the right track. Let's look at that idea some more." By listening to your instincts and stating what is going on for you, you allow the coachee to examine themselves and move to a different level of problem solving.

Here are some good ways to use your instincts in a coaching conversation:

Possible Employee Response	*Possible Follow-Up Responses*
I think that changing the report format will help matters.	I just got an adrenaline rush when you said that. What does your instinct tell you about this possible solution?
I want to tell accounting to bill our #1 client a late fee. What do you think?	I always trust my instinct when making important decisions about clients. What does your instinct say about this client?
The numbers look good for this project, but my gut tells me not to do this.	What *is* your gut telling you to do?

Build Awareness Before Action

Take a second and think about a professional golfer. Their task is to get the ball into the hole. That's what they get paid to do. But what do they constantly focus on? Their swing, which is the process they use to get the ball in the hole. They don't get paid to swing, but that's what they focus on. Hm, seems odd, right? Not really. Getting the ball in the hole is directly related to the quality of their swing. In other words, the quality of our end product is greatly affected by the process we follow to get there. Without a good process, accomplishing the task at hand is difficult. So how does this fit into coaching? Coaching helps us become aware of our process, in order to improve the actions we use while completing the task. Coaching focuses on Awareness Before Action because in coaching, the belief is that *how* we do something is just as important, if not more important, than *what* we do. As a manager, you need to constantly improve your process, as well as your employee's process, in order to hit the ball farther, make the shot cleaner, and get the ball into the hole. Your task as a manager is to help the organization meet its objectives. If you do that but leave a multitude of dead bodies in your wake, will you be successful in the long run? Probably not, because whether it is explicitly measured or not, managers are responsible for the process by which they accomplish their tasks.

We know, we know . . . you're busy and you just want to tick the next thing off your list. We also know that it's hard to think about process when you're fighting five fires at the same time. However, the best managers take time to think about the process, as well as the task. As a coach, your job is to ensure that the coachee has carefully thought about how their process is getting in the way of their success at the task. This awareness will help them create a better plan of action. Otherwise, the problem won't really get solved, and will just keep surfacing again and again.

So focus on Awareness Before Action when coaching; ask questions that focus on the process instead of fixing the problem.

TIP   Build Awareness Before Action

It's easy for both you and the coachee to want to jump to the solution and move on. However, as a coach, it's your job to help the coachee step back and gain some awareness about the situation before taking action. Spending ten minutes coaching about the process will save you hours later, so take the time now, rather than later, to get some distance from the problem and see what the real issues are. Ask a lot of questions during the first two stages of the W.I.N. B.I.G. model (Wonder about Root Cause and Investigate Wants) before moving on to the third stage (Name Possible Solutions), which is where you will look at the issue from a variety of angles. Doing this will help you stay unattached to one way of thought and will allow the coachee to look at the issue from another angle that they may have forgotten in their race to finding a solution.

Here are some good questions for helping a coachee gain awareness before jumping to the action:

Employee Comment	Typical Manager Response	Better Follow-Up Question
The IT department is delaying my work all the time.	How can you get them to move faster?	What else could be causing the delays?
I can't work with Sue. She's impossible.	How can you work around her?	What's the real issue in your dynamics with Sue?
I'm overwhelmed with my workload; it's too much.	What are you going to do about it?	What do you think is causing the work overload?

Remember, your job is not to fix the problem. Your job is to create a dialogue that allows the coachee to think about the process and find the solution to their own problem.

THE SEVEN TENETS OF COACHING ACTIONS

Mirror

When people need coaching, it's usually because they are too close to the situation to see clearly what's going on. In these cases, your job is to give the coachee the perspective they need to do their best thinking and find their own solution to a problem. This means that you have to act like a mirror and paint a picture of what is going on and then let the employee interpret or react to what they see. You may say, "So, Ty, on one hand I see you saying this is important and on the other I see you putting it off. . . . What do you make of that?" Sometimes your coachee may not want to hear or see the reflection; sometimes your coachee may be pleasantly surprised because they never saw the reflection themselves. Either way, mirroring allows your coachee to see their blind spot and take action to move forward.

Mirroring doesn't only refer to an individual's actions. Sometimes there is an obvious organizational issue that needs to be discussed, but instead everyone chooses to tiptoe around it. This causes frustration and a lack of trust. As a coach, your job is to name the pink elephant and mirror what you see happening in the organization. This isn't always easy to do; however, your coachee will trust you much more if you mirror it instead of ignoring it, especially if it's causing problems. Mirroring also gives them permission to talk about something they may be having a hard time talking about. Just by opening that access, they may find their own solution despite the pink elephant. If the subject had remained taboo, they would have stayed blocked to moving forward. Either way, whether organizationally or personally, hold up the mirror and explain to the coachee what you're seeing. It will unblock their blind spot and move them to new solutions.

TIP   Mirror

When mirroring, concisely and matter-of-factly explain what you heard and saw, without any judgment or condemnation. Then ask the coachee to interpret what is in the mirror. The key is to stay detached from their answer; you just want to act like a mirror for them, allowing them to see what you see. Doing this uncovers their blind spot. From this place of clarity, they can then move forward and find their own solution.

Here are some good ways to mirror while coaching:

"Let me tell you what I see going on. I see you saying that integrity is important to you in your work, but you're avoiding telling your subcontractor the truth about their quality of work to avoid a potential conflict with them. What do you notice about this situation?"

"What I notice is that you say you're not good at being a leader but you just told me a story in which everyone followed you and your ideas. What lesson do you learn from that story?"

"This is what I'm hearing. I hear you saying that on one hand you want a promotion and pay raise, and on the other hand saying that you don't want to take on any new responsibilities. What are your thoughts about a promotion?"

"You have not been happy or productive in your job since we changed our organizational strategy. What's going on?"

"I've noticed that whenever you head up a project that deals with Hector's department, you have a hard time getting it off the ground. Is there a connection there?"

Listen

Often, when we listen to someone, we're only partially listening, because we're thinking of our reply or judging their comments. We often miss what's in between their words, or even a key idea. As a coach, your job is to listen 100% to what the coachee is saying, as well as to what they're *not* saying—the ideas between their sentences. In addition to 100% focus, the key to good listening is to do it impartially. It's not your job to judge or analyze what the coachee is saying. Even if you disagree with, or even feel personally attacked by what the coachee may say, your role is to stay calm and unattached from their comments. This then allows the coachee to continue their personal learning, rather than become defensive about your personal judgments.

It's imperative that when you listen, you ask your questions based on what the employee says, not what you think they were going to say, your personal solution, or what you think is a great way to impress them with a clever question. So if Karen says, "Being pregnant has me worried that being a new mom will negatively affect my work load for the next year," a good follow-up coaching question would be, "Which parts of your work are you most concerned about?" rather than, "I forget, do you want a girl or boy?" The former follow-up coaching question focuses on the concerns that the coachee brought up and allows her to dig deeper to find her own solutions; the latter follow-up coaching question focuses on your personal interest in children and distracts the coachee from finding a solution. By listening at 100%, each follow-up question that you ask is peeling back the onion to dig deeper and learn more about the real issue at hand.

In addition to focusing on the words the person is saying, you also need to pay attention to the emotions the person is portraying and the body language the person is showing. Sometimes these three areas of listening can conflict, such as "I'm feeling great about this project," said with a heavy voice and twitching eyes. Your job is not to analyze the conflict; your job is just to notice it and let the coachee know what you're hearing. This is hard to do because listening takes time, and managers are taught to multitask and fix solutions quickly. But if you're not focused on listening 100% while coaching, you won't notice the conflicting words, emotions, and body language, and will potentially miss how the employee is in the way of their success.

By listening and allowing the coachee to feel heard, you're giving them the confidence that their words and ideas have merit and that they can figure things out for themselves.

TIP   Listen

The key to successful listening is to remove all distractions, sit back, and focus 100% on the coachee's words, emotions, and body language. You then want to tell the coachee what you heard in all three of these areas so they can use that information as they solve their own problem. So unplug yourself and focus 100% on what the person is saying, before you start coaching.

Here are some good ways to use all three parts of listening when coaching:

Possible Employee Response	*Possible Follow-Up Response*
I need more training on this topic.	Your eyes lit up when you said that you'd like more training. Your voice sounded excited about the idea.
I deserve a raise; I've worked 24/7 for you for 2 years.	You seem a little angry. You crossed your arms and lowered your voice when you said that you've worked 24/7 for me for 2 years and would like a raise.
I'm really confused.	You seem more than confused, you sound defeated and you're slumped in your chair. What's up?

Create Space

Creating space is one of the fundamental tenets of successful coaching. First of all, clear your area of all physical distractions. Turn off your phone, e-mail, IM, crackberry—anything that might pull your attention during the conversation. This seems almost too obvious to have to point out, but how many times have you been in the middle of a conversation with someone and they look at their ringing phone or dinging e-mail to see who is trying to reach them? When you are coaching, you need to focus 100% on your employee.

In addition to office interruptions, "create space" also means clearing your head and preparing yourself mentally for the coaching session. Just like a professional athlete prepares mentally before a race, a coach needs to prepare mentally for a coaching session. So if you're thinking about a big deadline or a problem at home, and are having a hard time switching gears, then get up, move your body, put on some music, do something to clear your head for the coaching session. Otherwise, you'll be doing your coachee a huge disservice because you won't be able to listen and focus on them 100%. The result? They'll be back in your office the next day with the same problem. Take some time now to save yourself time later. And if the coachee just appears in your office for an unexpected conversation, which is often the norm, do the same thing. If need be, tell the employee you want to focus on them completely and then ask for a few seconds to clear your head, grab a drink of water, stretch your legs . . . whatever it takes. Then start coaching from this place of cleared space.

Validate

If you're coaching someone, you're helping them deal with something that they have not dealt with on their own. It may not seem like a big deal to you, but it is for them; otherwise, they wouldn't be asking for your help. Validation can give people the confidence and motivation to get through their challenging situations.

TIP   Create Space

Creating space looks different to everyone. Some people prefer to coach in a different setting than the office, so that it's neutral territory and has less distractions. Others prefer to sit in the office but with their backs to the desk, so they're not distracted. Often coaching happens on the fly, so you may not be able to sit in a comfortable area reserved just for coaching, but be sure to create the space for you to listen and focus 100% on the employee.

Here are some possible ways to clear your space for a coaching session:

- Move away from your desk to another area.
- Turn off e-mail, IM, phones, computer, whatever latest gadgetry there is that might distract you, and close your door.
- If possible, give yourself a few minutes before the coaching meeting to focus your mind on the coachee, perhaps reviewing any notes you may have from a past coaching meeting.
- Play some music to switch gears in your head.
- Do some physical movement before the coaching session (jumping jacks, deep breaths, stretching, etc.) to get your blood flowing and your mind ready for a new topic.

When you validate during coaching, you are doing two things. First, you acknowledge to the person that you understand this is a big deal for them—you validate what it is they are going through or what it is that they have accomplished. Second, you validate something that they may not see in themselves such as how they are dealing, or have dealt with, the situation. For example: "Tonya, I just want to acknowledge that this is a big step for you, and I get that it can be intimidating . . . and I also want to recognize the fact that you're being really strategic and thoughtful in your planning and I see you as being up for the challenge."

The key to successful validating is to speak what you believe to be true regarding the coachee. It's important to remember that it's not about you and how they've impressed you. The validation is about them and their inner strength and power. Some good examples of validation are:

> "I know how hard you worked to get to where you are today. You committed to a plan, you stuck to it, and you asked for help along the way. Your tenacity is inspiring others. Congratulations!"

> "I get that this is a lot to take on, but I really see your inner strength as a leader coming out. I'm excited to watch you succeed with this project."

> "Although the project didn't turn out as you had planned, I saw you use clear communication and strong follow-up to get it to where it is today and I'm confident that it will go better next time."

Ask

Questions are the key to good coaching. Your coachee knows the answers to their problems. They have the Aptitude and the Available Resources, but are somehow lacking in the Attitude. So you don't need to solve the problem for them or tell them how to do it. You need to ask a lot of open-ended questions that will help them find their own answers for this and future problems.

See Chapter 3 for more about questions and how to:

1. Keep them open
2. Keep them advice-free
3. Keep them short and simple
4. Keep them thought-provoking
5. Keep them forward-focused

In Chapters 6 and 7, we have lists of great coaching questions you can ask during different stages of the W.I.N. B.I.G. model. The key is to stay curious and ask about whatever the coachee brings up.

TIP   Ask

Trust that you are asking the right questions. Even if you think you asked a bad question because the coachee didn't like it, it may be the perfect question for the coachee to mull over later. They may come back next week and say, "I thought about that question all weekend. It really gave me something to chew on about this issue." Likewise, if a question you ask doesn't seem to resonate with the employee, say something like, "That doesn't look like it was the right question . . . what question should I have asked you?" Invariably, they will come up with a great question that works for them. So stay detached from the outcome of the question. As long as it's open-ended and you're detached from the answer, it can be considered a good coaching question.

Feedback

An effective manager provides regular feedback to an employee. Why is this so important? So that the employee gets real-time information about their behavior and its effect on the organization, allowing them time to adjust their behavior to get different results. If the employee only heard feedback once a year at a performance review, they wouldn't have time to change their course of action. Consistent feedback allows them consistent growth, and improvement on a regular basis.

Feedback is a necessary step for coaching too. You may not do it during every coaching conversation, but there will be times when you take more control of the situation and give the coachee some feedback. When giving feedback, it's important to remember these basic rules:

- Be specific.
- Be focused on the *behavior* of the coachee.
- Focus on the impact the behavior had on the organization/team/ department.
- Help the coachee determine an alternative behavior that leads to an alternative effect.
- Speak in a matter-of-fact manner, without any judgment or condemnation.

Here is an example of giving feedback while coaching:

You: Mark, can I give you some feedback? What I've noticed is that when a client is late with their materials, you become frantic. You become short with your colleagues, cutting them off and not listening to their questions. Consequently, people avoid you and other work gets delayed. What do you think? [Pause for a response.]

Mark: I don't mean to get short with people, but I hate it when a client is late with their materials. It drives me up a wall. I feel like I'm the one clogging up the works and that everyone else is going to think I'm slacking. I guess when that happens I must get panicky and stop listening to people.

You: So it sounds like it's important for you to know that people think you're dependable.

Mark: Yeah, big time.

You: Well, what can you do to help slow yourself down and listen to people when clients are late?

Mark: Well, I could start off by taking a few minutes to get my act together so that I don't freak out.

You: And then?

Mark: I guess I could let the people involved know that the client materials are late. . . . I could send out an e-mail or go talk to people so that they are kept in the loop and people won't think it's me not doing my job. If I start to get panicky and cut people off, I could tell them that I am just stressed over the late materials. That might help.

You: Great! How will you remind yourself to do all of that the next time a client is late?

By giving Mark feedback, he learned about a behavior that is negatively affecting others in the department and found his own solution to changing his behavior in the future.

Celebrate

We know—who has time to celebrate anymore, with moving targets, new deadlines, and the next budget cut around the corner? It's hard for managers to keep their head above water, let alone take time to celebrate. However, we have seen how important celebration is to the coaching process. It allows people time to take stock of what they've accomplished. It lets them learn from their successes, hopefully to be used in future projects. And it's fun!

Celebration looks different to everyone. It doesn't have to be a splashy event, or even cost a penny. Some people want an announcement at a staff meeting, whereas others want a mass e-mail. Some people would love a handwritten note, a small gift, or a walk down the street for ice cream or coffee. Some people want it noted in their files or performance review. Others would love a half-day off. And some would just love a few minutes to brag about it with their manager! Even if it's only a ten-minute conversation, be creative and have fun. Let the person know what a great job they did and let them feel proud. That celebration feeling will then motivate them and give them the confidence to achieve their next goal.

> **TIP   Celebrate**
> Ask the coachee how they want to celebrate a victory. If they're unsure, give them some suggestions until they get excited about an idea. Be sure to honor your commitment to the coachee and do the celebration as soon as possible after the victory.

THE SEVEN TENETS OF COACHING TRICKS OF THE TRADE

Bottom Line

Bottom line, a manager's job is to be as effective and efficient as possible. One way to achieve this is to quickly get to the heart of the issue. This is harder for some people than for others. Extraverts tend

---

TIP   Bottom Line

It's OK to cut someone off and ask them to bottom line their
story in two to three sentences so that you can get to the real
issue. If the person seems truly upset that they can't finish their
story as planned, you could ask them to finish the story in one
minute, and then proceed to coach from there.

Here are some good ways to get to the bottom line:

Possible Employee Response	*Possible Follow-Up Question*
I'm having problems with Rachel.	So bottom line, in two to three sentences, what is the issue with you and Rachel?
Then he said this . . . so I said that . . . so then she said this . . .	[Jump in and interrupt.] It sounds like you must be going crazy with it all. We don't need to rehash the whole story. Just tell me in two sentences what's the heart of the problem.
You need to hear this. You're not gonna believe what happened when I tried to do this in the project . . .	[Jump in and interrupt.] Actually, just give me a three-sentence bottom-line summary so we can figure out your next steps.

---

to think while talking, so they need more time to talk before getting
to the bottom of what's going on. Introverts tend to process before
talking, so they may need some silence before they cut to the chase.
A coach's job is to get to the bottom line as quickly as possible, even
if it means cutting some people off before they finish their story.
This is necessary because often people think that "the story" is the real
issue, when most often it isn't. How many times have you listened

to someone tell a thirty-minute he-said, she-said story that could have been told in three minutes? Usually, the story can be reduced to a few sentences that describe the heart of the matter. Once you know the real issue, then the real coaching can occur.

Validating a person's emotions after a bottom-line response can help them move on even more quickly. "Wow, that sounds really frustrating" lets a person know you heard them and helps them prepare to move on.

Word Choice

As advertisers know, humans have both positive and negative reactions to certain words. Therefore, it's important to watch the words that you and the coachee use in the coaching conversation.

As a coach, you want to empower your coachee by using positive words that motivate, so avoid using the following words that can put the coachee in a downward cycle or on the defensive.

Why: Asking "why" can put someone on the defensive, shutting down the conversation instead of opening it up for creative solutions. See Chapter 3 for more about avoiding "why" when asking good coaching questions.

Possible Employee Response	Typical Manager's Response	Better Coaching Question
I missed my deadline this month.	Why did you do that again?	What could you do differently next month?
I don't want to work with Dan on this project.	Why not?	What are the biggest obstacles you see in working with Dan?

Should: Using the word "should" places your thoughts, judgments, and solutions on the coachee, instead of allowing them to create their own solution.

Possible Employee Response	Typical Manager's Response	Better Coaching Question
I missed my sales goals.	You should do more cold calls to improve your sales.	What's the effect of that?
I don't think I can do that.	You should rethink that because I think you can do it.	What would be different if you accomplished that?

Not/Can't: Using the words "not" and "can't" creates a negative spin to the coaching conversation, limiting your belief in the coachee's potential.

Possible Employee Response	Typical Manager's Response	Better Coaching Question
I screwed up on the new reporting format.	Formatting is not your thing. Let's look at other areas for your skills.	Bottom line, what's the biggest hurdle you face with formatting?
I can't follow the new IT system.	You're right. You can't. Let me give it to Joe instead.	I know it seems difficult right now. What can you do that would help you look at this task in a different light?

> **TIP   Word Choice**
>
> Here are some other red-flag words and some alternatives you can remind your coachee, to help them reframe the situation based on fact and not on fiction:
>
> Always (Maurice always makes me work late) ↔ Sometimes
>
> Everyone (Everyone in the department thinks this is a bad idea) ↔ Some people
>
> All the time (I mess it up all the time) ↔ Sometimes
>
> Never (Joe never praises me for a job well done) ↔ Rarely
>
> Can't (I can't do that) ↔ Won't/choose not to

Although it's important to watch the words you use when coaching, it's also important to listen to the words that the coachee uses. There are some words or phrases that are "red flags"—ones that limit the coachee's self-beliefs or keep them stuck in a conversation. Point out these red flags to help the coachee see their own blind spots and find a way to move forward.

Some of these red-flag words are: always, never, everyone, can't, and all. These words tend to be gross generalizations, based on a story and not on fact. When a coachee uses these words, they are usually living out a story in their head, instead of living out daily reality. For example, Deb says, "Maurice always makes me work late." It's doubtful that Maurice *always* does this to Deb; this is a story in Deb's head. More than likely, Maurice sometimes does it, but because it's a hot button for Deb, her story is that it *always* happens. Reminding Deb of this helps her reframe the statement and look at her hot button, rather than focusing on Maurice.

The key to doing this is to remain detached from their reply; because it's a story, they may get upset if you tell them that it's just a story in their head and not reality. So a good coaching response would be: "You used the word 'always' in that sentence. I'm guessing that Maurice sometimes makes you work late, not always. Stepping back and looking at the situation objectively, what's the real issue in this situation?" Once Deb sees that it is only sometimes, and not always, then she can unhook herself from Maurice and focus on how she can change her reaction to the situation. Once she starts focusing on herself, she can find her own solution to the problem instead of blaming Maurice for her problems.

Story Shift

Everyone has a story, or a perspective, on a situation. You could have ten people in the same room at the same time, involved in the same event, and you'd have ten different stories on what happened, none of which is totally right or wrong. However, the problem comes when we get attached to one story and think that *our* personal story is the only one, or the right one. As a coach, your job is to remind the coachee that there are many other perspectives about the problem at hand and that looking at the problem in a different perspective may help them find a solution they're looking for.

Changing perspectives isn't easy; most people have become successful at their job by knowing the answer, so they think their answer must be the right one. However, your job is to show the coachee all the different ways to look at a problem, helping them use a point of view they may not have thought about. Not only does this help them find their unique solution, but it also helps them use this technique to solve future problems.

Coach the Person

An effective manager focuses on coaching only the coachee, not anyone else that the coachee may mention during a conversation. When Melinda complains that Darcy never does her share of the work on a team project, it would be very easy to focus on Darcy instead of Melinda by asking, "Why do you think Darcy does that?" or "How do you think we can fix Darcy's habit?" Here's the news flash: There is nothing Melinda can do to change Darcy. The only

TIP   Story Shift

Being sensitive to the coachee's story is important. They may not realize that it's a story or perspective that they believe in. They may have told the story so many times that they think it's the absolute truth, instead of just one of many perspectives. So be matter of fact and concise when naming a story; don't judge it or give it any more importance than any other perspective.

Being playful and creative is important when trying to change perspectives; it helps people get out of their self-made box and find a different point of view. So don't be afraid to let loose when coaching someone on their story; the more attached they are to their story, the more they will need to look at different perspectives to find their solutions.

Here are some good ways to help someone shift their story, or perspective:

Possible Employee Response	*Possible Follow-Up Question*
I know Mary is causing the problem because she wanted her group to take the lead.	That's one perspective. There are lots of other ways to look at the cause of this problem. What else might be causing Mary to be late with her deliverables?
We're screwed . . . there's nothing we can do to get out of the situation.	Wow. What would President Lincoln tell you to do in this situation? Indiana Jones?
The Sr. Team just doesn't have a direction.	I can understand how you'd view it that way, *and* there are other ways to look at it. What are some other perspectives that might be equally true?

TIP   Coach the Person

Coaching the person in the room takes focus and commitment from both you and the coachee. If the coachee keeps bringing up the other person, you need to remind them that the issue is not the other person, but the coachee's response to the other person. The conversation could go something like this:

Wyatt: Tim didn't let me give my ideas for the new systems design at today's meeting.

You: How did you react to that?

Wyatt: I kept quiet; he didn't want to hear from me anyway, so why bother?

You: Let's look at you, not Tim. So what was the effect of you being quiet in the meeting?

Wyatt: I didn't really pay attention for the rest of the meeting. I just waited for the meeting to end.

You: So you tuned out and possibly missed some key points from the meeting. What's the effect of doing that on the organization?

Wyatt: No one got to hear my new idea that would save money and time for the IT team.

You: So what could you have done to be more effective with your and other's time in a meeting like that?

Wyatt: I could have been a lot more effective, if only Tim had kept quiet.

You: The issue is not Tim. You're never going to change him. However, you can change your reaction to this kind of situation. So take a deep breath and replay the meeting in your head. How could you have been more effective in today's meeting?

Wyatt: I could have spoken up when Tim asked for any other comments. I could have also spoken to him after the meeting about my ideas.

You: So what's the lesson learned?

Wyatt: I need to speak up when I have an idea. It helps me and it helps the organization.

> Focusing on Tim would only have kept Wyatt stuck in the complaining cycle. By focusing on his own reaction to Tim, Wyatt learned that his reaction affected not only him, but also the organization. He then created his own solution for future situations, which will make him more effective in the organization. Taking the focus off Tim allowed him to move forward in a positive way.

thing Melinda can do is change her reaction to Darcy and find her own solution that empowers her to do her best work, despite any issues that Darcy may bring to the team. The real issue is not Darcy; the real issue is that Melinda's hot buttons are being pushed in reaction to Darcy. For whatever reason, Melinda is letting those hot buttons stop her from moving forward.

Your job is to focus on the coachee and not get distracted by anyone that the coachee talks about. This allows the coachee to focus on themselves, how they get in their own way, and how they can get out of their self-imposed box. If you focus on the other person, you do a disservice to the coachee by keeping the focus off them and onto something over which neither of you has any control. If this happens, the employee is powerless to find a solution, and the problem will keep resurfacing.

Deal with Resistance

Generally, people want coaching because they want a change in a situation. However, some people don't even see that there's a problem, or aren't so keen on admitting that there is a problem. They are so wrapped up in their way being the right way, that they can't see the chaos around them. So when the topic of coaching comes up, they say that they have it all figured out and don't need any help. Or they may agree to talk about it, but then refuse to look at an issue in any other way than their own. When this happens, it's best to be curious about the resistance and stay unattached to the outcome of the session. This can be very frustrating for the coach, but very worthwhile if you can break through the resistance to the real issue that is blocking the coachee.

Self-management is the key when coaching someone who is resistant. You need to know how to manage your own buttons so that if the coachee accidentally pushes them when talking about their problem, you'll still be able to focus on them 100%. For example, if Charlene says, "I hate it when you edit my work for the annual report. It reminds me of being graded in school. I think my writing is fine and the report is good enough." If this was one of your hot buttons, you might then become defensive and start to plot ways to show Charlene just how bad her writing really is. As a result, you miss three minutes of what Charlene says next.

When your buttons get pushed by someone's resistance, just notice that your mind is wandering and try to bring it back to the

---

TIP   Deal with Resistance

When someone is resistant, your job is to be curious about the problem. Continue to ask open-ended, nonjudgmental questions and really listen and mirror back what you hear and see. Relax, breathe deep, and remember that the resistance is not about you as a coach. Don't take it personally; just trust your instincts and stay involved. Something good will come of it, whether during the meeting or when the coachee thinks about your questions at a later time.

Here are some good follow-up questions to ask when a coachee is resistant.

Possible Employee Response	*Possible Follow-Up Question*
I don't know the answer to that question.	That's fine. What do you know to be true about the problem at hand?
This is a waste of time.	What would have to happen for it to be a better use of your time?
It's pointless to talk about this.	OK. So what's the outcome of not dealing with it?

coachee. Take a deep breath and focus on their face and their mouth as they form the words. You could write down "defensive," for example, and draw a line through it so that you can get that button out of your head. Keep looking at the person until your focus on them returns to 100%. Be curious about their resistance and worry about yourself later, when you're done coaching.

Address Fears

One of the main reasons people don't accomplish a task or a goal is fear. Whether consciously or subconsciously, fear stops people in their tracks. They may not want a promotion because they're afraid they'll have to work longer hours and see the kids less. They may not want to lead a new project because they're afraid that they'll fail and look badly in front of their colleagues. These fears may not be rational or logical, but they can easily stop someone from moving forward. Your job is to help your coachee identify these fears and then look at them objectively. Often, when this happens, the coachee sees how illogical the fear is and is ready to move past it. Sometimes this can happen quickly; sometimes it takes longer as the coachee repeatedly hits the same barrier. Either way is fine. Your job is not to figure it out for them or move them through it quickly, but to shine the light on it for them and let them decide the next step.

Create Vision

It's easy to get caught up in the daily rat race of to-do lists—to just keep your head down and keep your nose to the grindstone. Sometimes, it's important to do this in order to meet a deadline. But doing this 24/7 without taking a breath of fresh air is not only soul-killing, it's ineffective. Every now and then you have to look up to see where you're going.

Every manager needs to know the organizational vision, so that they can steer their team in the right direction to achieve the company's goals. By the same token, every manager needs to know their individual team member's vision and goals as well. If Sharon wants

TIP   Fears

Many people have fears that prevent them from moving forward. They may have had these fears for a long time, so as a coach, you need to tread gently when dealing with them. For example, although it may seem irrational to you, a coachee's fear of failing at work and then being homeless on the street seems very real to them. Don't judge or mock the fear; just point it out and ask open-ended questions so the coachee can identify the fear and decide the next step. It may take some time for this process. Just stick with them and keep asking questions, trusting that they will identify their fear and find their own solution in their own time.

Here are some good ways to help a coachee identify a fear that is blocking them from moving forward:

Possible Employee Response	*Possible Follow-Up Question*
I can't take the promotion; I'm not ready yet.	What would be the worst thing that could happen if you took the promotion now? [They reply.] And then, what would be the worst thing to happen? [Keep going until they have completed the train of thought.]
I'd love to go to this training, but I don't think I'll be any good at it.	You sound a little intimidated. What scares you most about this training?
There is no way I could ever do what you do.	What if you could do what I did? What obstacles and fears would you have to overcome?

to become a manager, but is stuck doing administrative work for three years, she's not going to be motivated at work. If Clarence wants to get his MBA in two years, but is working sixty hours a week, he'll be disillusioned as he sees the time ticking away. It's important to know what your coachee's big-picture goals are, so you can help them move in that direction. If their current job and position help move them in the direction of their ultimate vision, they will continue working for you. Otherwise, they'll eventually move on to something that gets them closer to their goals, or they will R.I.P (retire in place) and become a resigned, unmotivated body on your team. They

---

TIP Create Vision

It's a good idea to use a map and/or know the constellations when sailing a boat around the world. By the same token, it's a good idea to know where your employees want to be in two to five years, so you can help them, and the rest of your team, successfully steer in the right direction.

Here are some good follow-up questions to use when helping a coachee develop their vision and goals:

Possible Employee Response	Possible Follow-Up Question
I love the people I work with, but find the work mundane.	What is your vision for yourself for the next five years? How is doing this work helping you get there?
I see the organizational vision, but I don't see how my work makes much difference.	What would it look like if your work was making a difference?
I'm not sure what the next step is for me within the organization.	What types of responsibilities do you want for your next step?

may not be able to articulate the details of their dream or vision yet; they may not have even thought about it at all. So give it time and don't rush it. Keep asking open-ended questions and allow them the time they need to conceptualize it. Remember, they'll be much more dedicated and excited at work if you help them achieve their goals. And you'll be more successful if they're more successful.

5

How Do I Use This Book?

When first learning to coach, many people sigh and say, "I don't have any idea what questions to ask—where do I start!?!" Don't worry—that's what the remainder of this book is for.

The following two chapters contain multiple sections with nothing but questions and tools to use when coaching.

- Chapter 6 contains specific sections of typical issues around which people often want coaching, such as, "How do I handle interpersonal problems?", "How do I handle conflicting priorities?", and "How do I handle a time-management issue?"
- Chapter 7 contains questions for you to ask as you work your way through any coaching situation by using the W.I.N. B.I.G. coaching model.

It may be helpful at this point to spend a few minutes flipping through Chapters 6 and 7 to familiarize yourself with the layout of the questions. Then return here for a quick overview of the steps to follow when using the book.

There are at least three different ways to use this book:

- As a resource to successfully coach employees and colleagues
- As a tool to give to employees to kick-off and/or support (not replace) the coaching when your time is limited
- As a tool to coach yourself through different situations

We'll start by examining how to use the book with others, and then as a self-coaching tool.

■ **Top Tips to Remember Before Starting to Coach**
Regardless of the topic or situation, keep these things in mind!

1. Clear Distractions
   - Turn off phones, pagers, e-mail, crackberrys, music, and other distractions.
2. Clear Your Mind
   - If possible, take a few minutes and clear your mind before you start coaching. Remember that this is about them, not you.
3. Ask Open Questions
   - Ask from a place of curiosity about the person, not from a place of figuring out or fixing the problem.
4. Listen
   - Listen to their whole answer—all that they are saying, all they are *not* saying, and all that their body-language is saying. Tell them what it is you are hearing and seeing.
5. Stay Curious
   - Don't approach with a preconceived idea of what the answer should be. Be open to what they say. Stay curious about how they are getting in their own way.
6. Go Deeper
   - Ask follow-up questions that pertain to their answers, not to your solutions.
7. Don't Know and Don't Fix It
   - Realize that you don't have to know the answer. Repeat: You don't have to know the answer to the question or how to solve the problem. Your job is to listen, not give advice.

8. Don't Get Attached
   - If you ask a question and it doesn't seem to work, ask another one. Or say, "What question *should* I ask you?"
9. Remember, Awareness *Before* Action
   - Build Awareness—W.I.N.
     - Wonder about Root Cause
     - Investigate Wants
     - Name Possible Solutions
   - Move to Action—B.I.G.
     - Build a Plan
     - Insure Action
     - Give Affirmation
10. Follow Up
   - Coaching is successful when some sort of action happens as a result of the conversation. Be sure to check in on progress, and hold the person accountable to their commitments.

USING THIS BOOK AS A RESOURCE TO COACH EMPLOYEES AND COLLEAGUES

Coaching can happen in one of two ways—a planned meeting, or coaching on the fly. If you scheduled a coaching meeting, spend a few minutes beforehand clearing your head and creating a good space for the conversation by eliminating all possible distractions. If a coaching situation just arises—as is most often the case for managers—you will have to ask the person if they want to spend some time talking about the situation, and once they agree, you'll need to clear away all distractions so that you can focus fully on the conversation. In either case, follow the steps outlined below to use this book to guide the conversation.

Set Up

1. *Determine Coachability*

   The first thing to do is to ask yourself if this is a situation that is appropriate for coaching. If it's not, don't start down the coaching path or everyone will end up frustrated. Coaching is appropriate when the person has the ability and most of the skills to handle the situation (Aptitude), but for some reason, they are in their own way of getting the job done (Attitude). (See Chapter 2 for more information on determining whether a situation is coachable.)

2. *Explain the Tool*

This book is a tool. Some managers feel uncomfortable using a book to help them have a conversation with their employees. We get that, but remember that people don't care that you use a tool to help you do your work—does anyone think it unusual because you use a computer? How about a budgeting form or a meeting agenda? People are fine with managers using tools; they just need to understand what the tool is and how you will use it. So don't just spring this book and all of these questions on people. As you begin the conversation, explain that you have been using this great new book to help you examine problems differently and tell the person you'd like to use it to help you guide your conversation. Explain that you will both be picking random questions from the book to help as, together, you think through the situation.

3. *Pick a Chapter*

Decide whether you will follow the questions from a Common Coaching Situation (i.e., Dealing with Interpersonal Issues) in Chapter 6, or if you will use the general questions from Chapter 7.

- Common Coaching Situation—If you are going to coach on a specific situation, turn to that situation in Chapter 6. You will notice that each of the situations has six sections of questions—one for each phase of the W.I.N. B.I.G. model. You'll start in the first phase, Wonder about Root Cause.
- General Coaching—If you are coaching on a general topic, turn to Chapter 7, which contains six sections of questions—one for each of the W.I.N. B.I.G. model. You'll start in the first section of Chapter 7, "Wonder about Root Cause."

Using the Book with Others

Set Up
1. Determine Coachability—Is coaching the best option?
2. Explain the Tool—Let people know what this book is.
3. Pick a Chapter—Specific Situations, Chapter 6; General Situations, Chapter 7

Build Awareness—W.I.N.

4. *Wonder about Root Cause*

   To start, randomly pick and ask a question from the "Wonder about Root Cause" section. Listen to what the person says without judging or giving advice. Follow up by asking a powerful question of your own that takes you deeper into their answer, or randomly pick another question from the section. Again, listen to their answer. If you notice a judgment or thought of your own popping up, breathe and focus on the person again. The goal here is *not* to ask all of the questions in the section, it's to understand the root cause of the situation at hand. When you think you both have a clear understanding of what is *really* going on underneath the issue, then move on to the "Investigate Wants" section. (See Chapter 3 for more information on all of the phases of the W.I.N. B.I.G. coaching model.)

   > During steps 4–9, be sure to listen and ask follow-up questions based on the person's answer. The questions in the book should be an "aid to," not a "replacement for" your own coaching questions that will naturally evolve based on the coachee's reply.

5. *Investigate Wants*

   Have the coachee randomly pick a question from the "Investigate Wants" section and ask the coachee the question. Listen to what

Remember, "Have you thought about trying . . . ?" is advice disguised as a question!

If a person's knee-jerk answer is, "I don't know," follow up with, "That's all right, just make up an answer." This gives the person freedom to explore, and can result in a very insightful response.

the person says. Do not let them problem solve (yet). Ask a follow-up question or pick a few more questions from the section, and earnestly listen to what the person is saying, with an awareness of what they are not saying. If the person feels stuck, then either ask another question from the section to keep the momentum going, or ask them what's making them feel stuck. When you think you are both clear on what the coachee wants from the situation and how they want to be in the situation, then move on to the "Name Possible Solutions" section.

6. *Name Possible Solutions*

Randomly pick a question from this problem-solving section. Remember that this phase of the W.I.N. B.I.G. model is all about generating possibilities in a fun way. The conversation should have the feel of a brainstorming session. Pick as many questions as you need, or ask your own, to get the person to think through multiple ways of solving the problem. When the coachee has chosen at least five possible solutions to the issue, it's time to move them to Build a Plan.

It's fine for you to add to the brainstorming, but don't be attached to your own idea. If the person responds to your suggestion in a less than favorable way, say something like, "Well, it looks like that might not work, but what *would* work?" You'll find this can often lead the coachee to some great solutions.

■ **Using the Book with Others**

Set Up
1. Determine Coachability—Is coaching the best option?
2. Explain the Tool—Let people know what this book is.
3. Pick a Chapter—Specific Situations; Chapter 6, General Situations, Chapter 7

Awareness
4. W-onder about Root Cause—Pick questions to get to the problem under the symptoms.
5. I-nvestigate Wants—Pick questions to help the person visualize.
6. N-ame Possible Solutions—Pick questions to help brainstorm and generate possible solutions.

Move to Action—B.I.G.

7. *Build a Plan*

Always start by asking the first two lead-in questions listed in this section: "Which of the possible solutions gets you closest to what you want?" followed by "Which one do you think you should pursue?" Then ask a series of questions from the section (or of your own) that help the coachee define what they want to do about the situation. When the coachee has clearly outlined their course of action, move to the "Insure Action" section.

> Do not skip these two steps of the process! Coaching without an action plan and accountability is not coaching; it's just a nice conversation!

8. *Insure Action*

Ask a series of questions from the accountability section that help you both clarify how the coachee will complete the commitment and what is needed from you to support them. Be sure to ask the closing question of this section, "So, in summary, what will you do by when, and how will I know?" Take the time for both of you to note the details in your calendar for follow up.

9. *Give Affirmation*

In this section, you (as the coach) respond to the questions or statements listed. It is the opportunity to give the person added motivation, bolster their confidence, and show your support. You can give affirmation at any point during the coaching process to acknowledge the person's efforts in the process. In addition to the "Give Affirmation" section, there are italicized questions scattered throughout all of the other five sections as a reminder to give affirmations throughout the entire coaching process and not just at the end of the conversation. If you or your coachee picks one of these, be sure to answer it as a way to validate the efforts your employee is making at that moment.

■ Using the Book with Others

Set Up	1. Determine Coachability—Is coaching the best option?
	2. Explain the Tool—Let people know what this book is.
	3. Pick a Chapter—Specific Situations, Chapter 6; General Situations, Chapter 7
Awareness	4. W-onder About Root Cause—Pick questions to get to the problem under the symptoms.
	5. I-nvestigate Wants—Pick questions to help the person visualize.
	6. N-ame Possible Solutions—Pick questions to help brainstorm and generate possible solutions.
Action	7. B-uild a Plan—Pick questions from this section that help create a thorough action plan.
	8. I-nsure Action—Pick questions from this section that set up an accountability structure.
	9. G-ive Affirmation—*You* answer questions from this section to recognize the person's strengths.

USING THE BOOK AS A TOOL TO GIVE TO EMPLOYEES TO KICK-OFF AND/OR SUPPORT COACHING

As we have said before, developing employees is a manager's responsibility and should be a focal point of their efforts. However, we are the first to admit that coaching takes time—a precious commodity for anyone in the business world. Naturally, there will be times when you have a major client meeting, and a coaching conversation with one of your employees is just not possible. There will also be times when an employee is dealing with a big issue that will take several coaching sessions. At those times, you can use this book as a tool to help move the coaching forward, even if you can't be a part of it. However, don't be fooled! This book will not, and cannot, replace actual coaching with an employee. But following these steps will allow you to use it as a way for employees to keep moving forward until you are back from that client meeting.

1. Determine Coachability

Before pushing this book at someone, ask yourself whether coaching is the best course of action for the situation. Coaching is appropriate when the person has the ability and most of the skills to handle the situation (Aptitude), but for some reason, they are in their own way of getting the job done (Attitude). Also ask yourself whether the person would benefit from working on some of the issues on their own, or if they should wait to have a conversation with you at a later time.

2. Explain the Tool

Tell the person about the book, and that you want to use it to start their thinking for a follow-up conversation with you at a later time. Or, if you are already coaching the person, tell them that you want them to use the book to move their thinking along until you talk again. Explain briefly how the book is set up, and then tell them to read and follow the directions for "Using This Book as a Tool to Coach Yourself." Ask them to keep notes of their thoughts to share with you when you get back together.

3. Pick a Chapter and/or Section

Give the person a specific area on which to focus. Do you want them to spend some time just in the "Wonder about Root Cause" section, or do you want them to work all the way through a specific topic and come back and share their action plan? It will depend largely on the employee, how often you have coached them on other issues, and the situation with which they are currently dealing.

4. Set a Time for Follow Up

Do not hand over the book without setting a time for a follow-up meeting. The timing will depend on the situation at hand, but it should be sooner than later. If the employee has come to you, chances are it is an important issue for them. Situations that call for coaching typically distract employees from focusing completely on their other tasks, so try to meet with them within the week, at the latest.

5. Hold the Follow-Up Meeting and Continue Coaching

At the follow-up meeting, start by asking the person to share with you the insights that they gleaned as a result of their work. Keep the book in front of you, and ask more questions as you go along. After the person has shared, work through the remaining phases of the W.I.N. B.I.G. model. If the person has worked all the way through their situation, be sure to spend some time in the final two phases; "Insure

> Giving an employee this book without setting up a time to meet for discussion is a copout—don't do it! Meet and discuss—sooner than later!

Action" and "Give Affirmation" by discussing questions from those sections. Close the meeting by thanking the person for working on their own, and reminding them of your support as they move forward.

Using the Book as a Tool to Supplement Coaching

1. Determine Coachability—Is coaching the right option here?
2. Explain the Tool—Tell them to read "Using This Book as a Tool to Coach Yourself."
3. Pick a Chapter and/or Section—Decide what part(s) of the W.I.N. B.I.G. model they will work on.
4. Set a Time for Follow Up—Find or make a time to meet in the near future.
5. Hold the Follow-Up Meeting and Continue Coaching— Listen to what they have determined and pick up with the coaching.

USING THIS BOOK AS A TOOL TO COACH YOURSELF

Obviously, for coaching to be most effective, a coach needs to be involved. Otherwise, it would be like going to the dentist without a dentist—an option that might sound good to some people, but one that would result in not-so-great teeth. However, because it's not possible, or necessary, to go to the dentist every day, we do our own dental-hygiene routine between visits. It's similar with this book. When it's not possible to talk with your coach, or when you're in a situation in which you don't have a coach, follow the steps below to help you step back and look at your situation differently and generate a plan for success.

Set Up

1. *Determine Coachability*

   The first thing to do is ask yourself whether this is a situation that is appropriate for coaching. If it's not, don't start down the coaching path. Use this book for situations in which you keep banging your head against the same wall—you have a good deal of ability and most of the skills to handle what's going on (Aptitude) but for some reason you seem unable to change the situation (Attitude).

2. *Get Prepared*

   To self-coach, you need to clear distractions that will prevent you from focusing. Find a quiet spot where you'll have a good chunk of time to sit and reflect. Write down your thoughts and plans. Keeping all of the notes from different coaching sessions in one spot can be very useful. Take the time to reread them to remind yourself of the insights. It's amazing how quickly an insight can disappear from our mind.

3. *Pick a Chapter*

   Decide whether you will follow the questions from a Common Coaching Situation (i.e., Dealing with Interpersonal Issues) as presented in Chapter 6, or if you will use the general questions from Chapter 7.

   Keep a journal of your coaching thoughts and periodically review your insights —you'll be amazed at how much you're learning!

   - Common Coaching Situation —If you are going to coach on a specific situation, turn to that situation in Chapter 6. You will notice that each of the situations has six sections of questions— one for each phase of the W.I.N. B.I.G. model. You'll start in the first phase, "Wonder about Root Cause."
   - General Coaching—If you are coaching on a general topic, turn to Chapter 7, which has six sections of questions—one

for each phase of the W.I.N. B.I.G. model. You'll start in the first section of Chapter 7, "Wonder about Root Cause."

■ Using the Book to Coach Yourself

Set Up
1. Determine Coachability—Is coaching the best option?
2. Get Prepared—Grab a journal and find a quiet spot.
3. Pick a Chapter—Specific Situations, Chapter 6; General Situations, Chapter 7.

Build Awareness—W.I.N.

4. *Wonder about Root Cause*

   Randomly pick a question from this section. Spend some time writing down your thoughts about the question. After a minute or two, follow up by randomly picking and writing about one to three more questions from the section. The goal is not to work through all of the questions in the section. Before moving on to the next section, spend a few minutes skimming over what you've written and make a few notes about what it is that you've discovered in this section. When you think you have a clear understanding of what is really going on underneath the issue, then move on to the "Investigate Wants" section.

   > It is easy to get absorbed into writing a lot in the first section and then lose steam for the process. If you think that will happen to you, set some clear time limits for each section.

5. *Investigate Wants*

   Randomly pick a question from the "Investigate Wants" section and spend time journaling about the answer. Avoid problem solving at this point. Answer a few more questions from the section. If a question doesn't seem to work for you, choose another one, or make up a question that *does* work for you and answer it instead. When you think you are clear on what your wants and vision are for the situation, move on to the "Name Possible Solutions" section.

6. *Name Possible Solutions*

Randomly pick a question from the "Name Possible Solutions" section. Remember that this phase of the W.I.N. B.I.G. model is all about generating possibilities in a fun way. Don't take it too seriously—you are brainstorming and there are no bad ideas! It is vital here that you don't stop after answering just one question. Pick as many questions as you need to think through multiple ways of solving the problem. You should have no less than five possible solutions to the issue. When you do, it's time to "Build a Plan."

> Keep working through the process . . . awareness without action is just wasted introspection.

Using the Book to Coach Yourself	
Set Up	1. Determine Coachability—Is coaching the best option?
	2. Get Prepared—Grab a journal and find a quiet spot.
	3. Pick a Chapter—Specific Situations, Chapter 6; General Situations, Chapter 7
Awareness	4. W-onder about Root Cause—Answer several questions, then review your answers and summarize your key discoveries.
	5. I-nvestigate Wants—Answer several questions that will help you clearly see what outcomes you desire for the situation.
	6. N-ame Possible Solutions—Answer several questions that will help you generate at least five ways of dealing with the situation at hand.

Move to Action—B.I.G.

7. *Build a Plan*

Start by asking yourself the first two lead-in questions listed in this section: "Which of the possible solutions gets you closest to what you want?" followed by "Which one do you think you should pursue?" Then pick a series of questions from the section that helps you define what it is you want to do about the situation. When you have clearly outlined a course of action, move to the "Insure Action" section.

> Insight without action is simply introspection. Answer the questions that help you build a solid plan to move forward.

8. *Insure Action*

This is a very important step when you are self-coaching. To successfully complete the actions you've outlined in "Build a Plan," you will need support—someone to hold you accountable and cheer you on when needed. This section has additional questions to use when you are self-coaching. If you are working in Chapter 6, they are listed at the beginning of the chapter on p. 147. In Chapter 7, they are listed at the end of the Insure Action section on p. 217. Pick a series of questions from this section to help develop an accountability structure.

9. *Give Affirmation*

Most people want to skip this section. Don't! There is nothing wrong with taking the time to give yourself an occasional pat on the back. At the end of the Give Affirmation" section in Chapter 7 (p. 221), there are additional questions to use when you are self-coaching. Choose at least two questions from the list and write the answers in your journal. Close by transferring any necessary notes from your journal to your calendar, and then go put that plan into action.

> Take the time to acknowledge what you are learning —give yourself the credit you deserve.

■ Using the Book to Coach Yourself

Set Up	1. Determine Coachability—Is coaching the best option? 2. Get Prepared—Grab a journal and find a quiet spot. 3. Pick a Chapter—Specific Situations, Chapter 6; General Situations, Chapter 7
Awareness	4. W-onder about Root Cause—Answer several questions, then review your answers and jot a summary of your key discoveries in this section. 5. I-nvestigate Wants—Answer several questions that will help you clearly see what outcomes you desire for the situation. 6. N-ame Possible Solutions—Answer several questions that will help you generate at least five ways of dealing with the situation at hand.
Action	7. B-uild a Plan—Answer the listed lead-in questions, then choose a few more to develop a thorough plan of action. 8. I-nsure Action—Answer several questions at the end of this section specified for self-coaching. 9. G-ive Affirmation—Answer at least two questions at the end of this section specified for self-coaching.

6

W.I.N. B.I.G. Questions for Specific Coaching Situations

If you haven't already done so, you may want to take a look at Chapter 5, "How Do I Use This Book?" You may also want to skim Chapter 7 to see how it differs from Chapter 6.

Whereas Chapter 7 offers general coaching questions that can be used in any situation, this chapter is divided into eleven sections—one section for each of the most common work issues that managers face on a regular basis:

- Interpersonal Problems (page 149)
- Motivation (page 153)
- Time Management (page 158)
- Dealing with Conflict (page 162)
- Clarifying Goals (page 167)
- (Lack of) Available Resources (page 171)
- Developmental Opportunities (page 175)
- Life Balance (page 180)
- Conflicting Priorities (page 184)
- Delegation (page 189)
- Increasing Confidence (page 193)

Use the questions in these sections to help guide you through a coaching conversation on these specific topics. For example, if your employee is coming to you for help with Time Management or Conflicting Priorities, then you'd turn to that section of this chapter and start coaching by using the specific questions listed. That doesn't mean that the questions in the "general question" section of Chapter 7 wouldn't work as well. It just means that these questions were written specifically to help you coach through each of these eleven workplace issues.

In each of the eleven sections, you'll see each of the stages of the W.I.N. B.I.G. coaching model. There are ten questions in each stage (some have follow-up questions). These are by no means all of the possible questions to ask in these areas, just a few to get the ball rolling. The questions should serve as an aid-to, not a replacement-

> Remember to keep this light and fun—coaching does not have to be a long and laborious process!

for coaching questions that come from your own curiosity. Your goal is not to ask all ten questions in each section! Have your coachee pick a number between one and ten and use that question to start the dialogue in that section. Follow up with questions of your own, pick another number from the list, or pick a question from the relevant sections of Chapter 7. Answer enough questions until you get all of the information you need in that section of the W.I.N. B.I.G. model, and then move on.

There is one italicized "Give Affirmation" question in each of the sections. If you or your coachee picks this one, it is up to the coach (that's you!) to answer it in order to validate the coachee's efforts. Again, these questions should serve as a reminder for you to give affirmation. Feel free to change them, and be sure to give affirmation throughout the process, not just when one of the questions is chosen.

Before you use this chapter, you might want to review the stages of the W.I.N. B.I.G. model. The summary below will apply to each of the eleven topics, so refer to it for each topic that you're coaching on.

WONDER ABOUT ROOT CAUSE—DISCOVERY

In the first step of coaching, "Wonder about Root Cause," your job is to ask questions that will encourage your employee to curiously examine underlying causes for the issue presented.

In this chapter, be prepared to switch on a dime at any point during the "Wonder about Root Cause" stage. You may determine, for example, that the real issue beneath someone's motivation problem is an interpersonal problem. If that's the case, try switching to that specific section, or to the general questions in Chapter 7. Also, in this chapter, "Wonder about Root Cause" is sometimes just a question or two to validate that you are in the right place. For example, look at "Development Opportunities." If you are coaching someone because you think they want or they've said they want development opportunities, then you already know the root cause and can move them to "Investigating Wants" fairly quickly. Use the "Wonder about Root Cause" section as a way to ensure that you are coaching about the real issue, and then move on.

> In this section, continue probing deeper until you get to the root cause. Follow-up questions are important, as are statements that keep the coachee engaged, such as "Tell me more," "Say more about that," and "What else?"

INVESTIGATE WANTS—VISION

In this section, your goal is to help the employee clarify what they really want from the situation and *whom they want to be as they*

> If the person answers with an, "I don't know," say "That's cool, just make it up." The answer may prove to be the right one.

move in that direction. Make an effort to remember their answers, because you'll want to refer back to them when you get to problem solving.

You might start this section off by saying something like:

- It seems like we have a good idea of what's going on, and obviously that's not the way you want it. Let's talk about that for a minute. How do you want this situation to be?
- Wow, so you are up against some pretty big stuff. Let's talk about what it would look like if things were different. Pick a number between one and ten . . .

NAME POSSIBLE SOLUTIONS—PROBLEM SOLVING

The goal of this stage is to help the person become aware of the multitude of possible solutions and choices they have as they move toward their vision. This should have the feel of a brainstorming session. Do not let them get into the nitty-gritty details of action planning (the next section) until you have generated a number of possible solutions.

You might start by saying something like:

- You've got a great idea of who you want to be in this situation. Now let's look at some ideas about how to get there. So, based on what you just said that you want . . . [pick a question].

> Again, this is a great place to encourage the coachee to elaborate. Use statements like, "Tell me more," "Say more about that," and "What else?" to expand the conversation.

Remember to ask all of these questions *based on what they said they wanted* in the "Investigate Wants" section.

- It sounds like if all of that happened, you'd be in a great place. Let's talk about the ways you could make it happen. Pick a number between one and ten. Based on what you just said you wanted the situation to look like . . .

BUILD A PLAN—ACTION

Your goal in this stage is to help the coachee devise a realistic plan that gets them where they want to go in a doable manner and time-frame. Your questions can get more specific as you help drive the person toward a real action plan.

Start this section by asking the first two questions to help the person narrow and choose from the possible solutions they have just developed.

You might start with something like:

- You've got some great possibilities you could pursue. Now let's choose one and look at the details of how to make it happen. [Go to the two lead-in questions.]
- Cool, lots of options, huh? Why don't we narrow them down and talk about how to really make one happen? [Go to the two lead-in questions.]

The questions in this section should all pertain to the solution chosen as a result of the first two lead-in questions of this section.

Always start this section with these questions:

- Which of the possible solutions gets you closest to what you want?
- Which one do you think you should pursue?

Continue to check in on this solution by asking something like, "In what ways does this plan get you what you said you wanted in this situation?"

INSURE ACTION—ACCOUNTABILITY

Your goal here is to help the employee hold true to their commitments by establishing an accountability system. Be sure to take notes for yourself. You will be responsible for holding this person accountable, so you will need to follow through on your commitments.

End this section with the given close-out question:

- "So, what are you going to do by when, and how am I going to know?"

You might start this section by saying something like:

- OK, you've got a great plan, and I also know you have a lot of other things waiting for you back on your desk. Let's spend a few minutes talking about how we can make sure this doesn't get buried by something else. Pick a number between one and ten . . .
- This all sounds great. I really want to see you do this, so I want to help hold you accountable to what it is you say you want to achieve. Pick a number between one and ten . . .

Your intent here is not to be a nag or a micro-manager. Your intent is to help keep the employee's commitments in the forefront of their mind so that they can be successful. Ask your questions with that intent and with that mindset.

If You Use This Book on Your Own

If you are using this book on your own, answer any of the questions listed in the "Insure Action" section of your selected topic area, but be sure to come back here and answer these as well:

1. Who will help hold you accountable to your plan?
2. What do you need from that person in order to be successful?
3. What physical object (a sticky note on your computer, a rubber band on your water bottle, etc.) can you use to help remind you of your plan?
4. What will you do, by when, and how will you let someone know you've done it?

GIVE AFFIRMATION—VALIDATE

Your purpose in this section is to validate the goals, efforts, and plans that the person is putting forth and to validate the strengths or qualities that you see, think, or know will make them successful as they move forward. [In this section you (the coach) answer the questions.]

You could start by saying something like:

- This is great. You've got a solid plan. I just want to take a second and point out what you've done here . . .
- OK, before we end, I want to take a second to validate the effort you've made. Pick a number between one and ten . . .

These questions are meant to be starters. You may want to add some of your own as you acknowledge the person for what they've done, who they are, and what they've committed to do. Real validation has to come from *you*, not a book!

If You Use This Book on Your Own

If you are using this book on your own, answer any of the questions listed in the "Give Affirmation" section of your selected topic area, but be sure to come back here and answer at least two of these as well:

1. How is all of this helping you move toward becoming the person that you want to be?

2. What are three things in all of this that you should give yourself a "pat on the back" for?

3. Pick an animal you respect. How are you like that animal right now?

4. In what ways are you proud of yourself for working through this issue?

5. What's one positive thing that you know is true about yourself right now?

6. What qualities would your best friend say you are exhibiting right now?

7. In what ways would you stand out from a crowd right now?

8. Who is one of your heroes? In what way are you like them right now?

9. In what ways are you being "the person you want to be" right now?

10. What's something that you are doing/plan on doing in all of this that is a stretch for you?
    - How does that stretch excite you?

You can also answer as many of the questions as you'd like from the ten listed in each of the eleven sections by replacing "this person" with "you." Go ahead, you deserve it.

■ INTERPERSONAL PROBLEMS ■

Wonder about Root Cause

1. What's the effect of not dealing with this issue?

2. What needs to be said here that's not being said?

3. What's your contribution to the problem?

4. What's the real reason you are having a hard time working with this person/these people?

5. If this situation were an onion, what's the problem one layer under this layer?

6. What would your best friend say is going on in this situation?
   - That's one way of looking at this situation. Name three other people. What would each of them say is going on in this situation?

7. What are you most afraid of in this situation?

8. Give Affirmation: *How is this person stretching out of their comfort zone right now?*

9. What's hindering you from dealing with this person/these people?

10. How is this situation misaligned with who you want to be as a person?

Investigate Wants

1. If this situation was resolved, what would be different in your life?
   - What would that get you?

2. If you were writing a movie about this relationship, how would you write the ending?

3. How would this have to play out for you to feel good about it?
   - How would you have to act?

4. What skills do you have the opportunity to develop in this relationship?

5. What would be the fairy-tale ending to working with this person/ these people?

6. How could you use this relationship to help you move in the direction of your goals?

7. What would *real* resolution look like?

8. What's important for you as a person as you move toward resolution?

9. Give Affirmation: *How is this person being courageous now?*

10. How would someone you disrespect play this out?
    - What do you like and dislike about that option?

Name Possible Solutions

1. How would a child solve this problem?

2. What haven't you tried that you know would be helpful?

3. What's the win-win solution for everyone involved?

4. How would the Three Stooges handle this interpersonal problem?

5. Give Affirmation: *How is this person being true to themselves right now?*

6. In the book of *My Perfect Life,* how would this relationship play out?

7. If this group of people/person was a rock band, what would be different?
   • Country Western Band? Hip Hop Group?

8. What would you do in this relationship, if your life depended on it?

9. How does your decision fit with what's important to you?

10. What conversations would you need to have to get you what you said you want?
    • What type of person would you want to be during these conversations?

Build a Plan

• *Which of the possible solutions gets you closest to what you want?*
• *Which one do you think you should pursue?*

1. So what do you need to do to get what you want in this relationship?

2. How might this solution cause ripples with others?
   • How will that affect your plan?

3. What's the best time and way to go about implementing this plan?

4. How will you communicate this plan to others?

5. Give Affirmation: *What three positive qualities is this person showing right now?*

6. How are you going to get other people on board with your plan?

7. What kind of support or resources do you need to ensure success?
   - How will you go about getting it?

8. How will you know that this solution is a success?

9. What's the biggest obstacle to implementing your decision?
   - What safeguards do you want to build in to ensure success?

10. What kind of person do you want to be as you resolve this situation?
    - How do you ensure that shows up in your plan?

Insure Action

1. What should I do if I don't see you following through?

2. Whom else could you talk to who will hold you accountable?

3. When you think of your priorities, what needs to shift as you add this to your plate?

4. What's the potential impact of you not following through on your commitment to resolving this situation?

5. What's the most likely way you'll sabotage your success?
   - How do you want me to be with you when I see that happening?

6. Give Affirmation: *How is this person displaying new, positive attitudes right now?*

7. What support (or direction) do you need from me?

8. If you can't tie a string on your finger, what else could you do to remember to keep your commitment?

9. How will you celebrate your success both individually and as a group?

10. What's the potential effect of not doing this, both on yourself and on the other person/group?
    - How are you going to remember that as you move forward?

Final Question:

So, what are you going to do by when, and how am I going to know?

Give Affirmation (*Answered by the Coach:* Choose One)

1. What do you admire about this person in this situation?

2. What do you see them tackling in a new way?

3. Whom do you see them working with in a new way?

4. How are they behaving differently now than in the past?

5. What struggles do you see this person overcoming?

■ MOTIVATION ■

Wonder about Root Cause

1. So what's really going on?

2. What's the biggest reason you can't get excited about this situation?

3. What is it about this situation that makes it difficult to get/stay motivated?

4. On a scale of one to ten, how energized are you about this situation?
    - What's that about?

5. How is this similar to other times in your life when you haven't been motivated?

6. In what ways are you the biggest obstacle to your own motivation?

7. In what ways are you not being the person you'd like to be in this situation?

8. What's holding you back from getting more motivated?

9. Which of your buttons are really getting pushed in this situation?

10. Give Affirmation: *In what ways is this person inspiring you right now?*

Investigate Wants

1. What would have to be happening in this situation for you to be really jazzed about it?

2. Give Affirmation: *In what ways is this person going after what they want right now?*

3. On a scale of one to ten, how energized are you about this?
   - What would have to be happening for it to be two notches higher?

4. What are the things that make a situation motivating to you?
   - What would have to be happening here for those things to exist?

5. What would it take for you to feel really successful in this situation?

6. How would you like people to describe you as you move forward in this?

7. If you could do anything you wanted in this situation, what would you do?
   - What would that get you?

8. What happens if you never get motivated about this? And then what happens? What's the learning from that?

9. What kind of animal do you want to be like as you resolve this issue?
   • What would that get you?
   • How could you incorporate those traits when resolving this?

10. What is your vision for yourself in the next two years?
    • How does that affect how you want to resolve this situation?

Name Possible Solutions

1. How would Indiana Jones [insert any character] tackle this issue?

2. What are some of the possible ways to get motivated about this?

3. Who motivates you to keep going when the going gets tough?
   • What do you need to ask that person to help you succeed?

4. If you had a clean slate and could start from scratch, what would you do?

5. What's a solution to this that you would hate?
   • What's the opposite of that solution?

6. What kind of person do you have to "be" to get motivated? What do you have to do to get motivated?

7. What's the solution you've been too afraid to try? What will this solution get you?

8. Give Affirmation: *If you were giving an award to this person right now, what would it be for?*

9. What's a solution that would keep you from being stuck in a rut?
   • What aspects of that solution appeal to you?

10. What conversations would you need to have to get motivated?
    - With whom do you need to have these conversations?

Build a Plan

- *Which of the possible solutions gets you closest to what you want?*
- *Which one do you think you should pursue?*

1. How will doing this affect you as a person?

2. What do you need to know about your solution that you don't already know?

3. What concerns you most about your decision?

4. What steps do you need to consider to ensure that this decision fits with your values?

5. How can this be a motivating plan?

6. What do you need to include to ensure that you're happy about this decision in five years?

7. What happens if you lack motivation again in a week?

8. How do you make this plan as easy as possible?

9. Give Affirmation: *What do you see this person overcoming to build this plan?*

10. What do you have to do to get there? Who do you have to "be" to get there?

Insure Action

1. What are you committed to trying?

2. What'll motivate you when the going gets tough?

3. How will you remind yourself to do this on a regular basis?

4. What do you have to say no to, to make this happen?

5. Who motivates you?
   • What can you apply from this person that will motivate you to keep going forward?

6. Give Affirmation: *What new attitudes is this person showing right now?*

7. What'll motivate you to ask for help, if needed?

8. What's important about honoring this commitment?

9. What's in it for you if you succeed at this?
   • How can you celebrate when you get there?

10. At what stage of a project do you normally lose motivation?
    • What will you do differently for this project?

Final Question:
   So, what are you going to do by when, and how am I going to know?

Give Affirmation (*Answered by the Coach:* Choose One)

1. What strengths do you see in this person right now?

2. What do you see in the person that they might not see in themselves?

3. How is this person in alignment with what's important to them?

4. What about this person lets you know they'll succeed?

5. In what ways should this person be proud of themselves?

■ TIME MANAGEMENT ■

Wonder about Root Cause

1. What do you think is *really* causing this situation?

2. Bottom line: What's the biggest hurdle you're facing with your current time management situation?

3. What are your most important priorities?
   - How are those reflected/not reflected at work?

4. What would you have to say no to in order to have the time you need?
   - What kind of effect would that have?

5. What's your contribution to the problem?

6. How do your projects manage you, instead of you managing your projects?

7. Give Affirmation: *How is this person inspiring others right now?*

8. If you had all the time in the world, how would you chunk it out?

9. How would your worst enemy describe this situation?
   - What would they say is going on?
   - What's true about that?

10. How is this like another situation you've experienced?
    - What did you learn from that situation?
    - How can you apply those lessons to this situation?

During this stage, be prepared to switch to another section of this book. Time management issues are typically caused by something else.

Investigate Wants

1. What qualities do you have to demonstrate to achieve better time management?

2. If you had a magic wand, how would the situation look?
   - How could you use this to help you move in the direction of your goals?

3. If you had no clock to watch, what would you do in this situation?

4. Give Affirmation: *How do you know this person will succeed in solving this issue?*

5. What would it take for you to feel really successful with your time management?

6. What do you like about not having enough time?
   - What's another way you could get that?

7. How do you want to spend your time?

8. How would you be if you were always "in the flow"?
   - What would that get you?

9. If you got what you wanted in this situation, what would you have?

10. Take a step away from the issue at hand. How do you want to be as a person?
    - What would the desired outcome look like in that light?

Name Possible Solutions

1. What are some ways you could go about getting what you want?
   - What's another?

2. What are some quick solutions?
   - What do you dislike about those options?

3. There are twelve solutions to any problem: What are three of them?

4. Where haven't you looked for a solution yet?

5. What would you do if you had free reign in this situation?
   - Where will this solution lead?

6. What's the hardest way to solve this time-management problem?
   - What's the easiest way to have this turn out the way you want?

7. Give Affirmation: *What new skills is this person showing right now?*

8. What haven't you prioritized that you know you need to?

9. If you only had time to work on two top-priority projects, what would they be?
   - What's that about?
   - How does that affect your potential solution?

10. What do you have to say no to in order to gain more time?
    - How can you go about doing that?

Build a Plan
- *Which of the possible solutions gets you closest to what you want?*
- *Which one do you think you should pursue?*

1. What's the most important part of the new plan to execute?

2. How would you pull all this together to make it a priority?

3. What support or resources do you need to ensure success?
   - How will you go about getting it/them?

4. What could stop you from moving forward on your decision?
   - What safeguards do you want to build in to ensure success?

5. How will you communicate this plan, and its priority, to others?

6. How are you going to get other people on board with your plan?

7. Give Affirmation: *What do you see this person tackling in a new way?*

8. How will this decision impact your future?

9. How do you ensure that this decision fits into how you want to be as a person?

10. If you did this, how will it affect your stakeholders?
    - How do you use this information to create your plan?

Insure Action

1. What are you committed to having happen here?

2. What do you have to say no to, to make this plan happen?

3. How can I run defense for you?

4. What would you have to *stop* doing to successfully execute this plan?

5. Give Affirmation: *What type of animal does this person remind you of right now?*
    - *What qualities of that animal is this person showing now?*

6. How will you stay energized about this after a month?

7. What's the best way for you to circle back to me on this?

8. What's in it for you if you succeed at this?

9. What do you need from me to be successful?

10. At what stage of a project/plan do you normally lose motivation?
    - What will you do differently for this goal?

Final Question:

So, what are you going to do by when, and how am I going to know?

Give Affirmation (*Answered by the Coach: Choose One*)

1. What do you see them doing that is a step forward?

2. How are they behaving differently now than in the past?

3. What new habits is this person implementing?

4. How is this person being a leader right now?

5. What makes this person stand out from the crowd?

■ DEALING WITH CONFLICT ■

Wonder about Root Cause

1. What is it about this conflict that "makes you lose sleep"?

2. On a scale of one to ten, how much does this conflict distract you from your other work?
   • What's that about?

3. Give Affirmation: *How is this person moving outside their comfort zone right now?*

4. In what ways are you not being the person you'd like to be in this situation?

5. What's underneath the conflict?

6. How would an outsider look at this conflict?

7. Which of your buttons are really getting pushed in this conflict?

8. What do you value that's not being respected in this situation?

9. What might be your blind spot in this conflict?
   - [If they say, "I don't know," then a good reply would be, "Make it up."]

10. What do you want *for* the other person/people in this situation?

Investigate Wants

1. If you were a screenwriter, how would you write the ending of this conflict?

2. What do you value that you're not willing to compromise as you resolve this?

3. How would you like people to describe you as you resolve this?

4. Give Affirmation: *How is this person overcoming a hurdle right now?*

5. What does the desired end state look like for you?

6. When you are eighty-five years old, what do you want people to say about you?
   - How does that affect how you want to resolve this conflict?

7. If you could do anything you wanted in this situation, what would you do?

8. What would it take for you to feel really successful when resolving this conflict?

9. How would someone you disrespect play this out?
   - What do you like and dislike about that option?

10. How would this have to play out for you to feel good about it?
    - How would you have to act for that to happen?

Name Possible Solutions

1. How would a teenager handle this conflict? A wizard? A whale?
   - What do you like and dislike about these perspectives?

2. What solution would ratchet up the conflict? What solution would be the "doormat solution"?
   - What appeals to you about those solutions?

3. What's the win-win solution?
   - How could you make that happen?

4. How would Marie Antoinette [insert any character] tackle this issue?

5. What could you do to bring everything back into alignment?

6. What solution would embarrass you the most?
   - What's the opposite of that solution?

7. What's the solution you've been too afraid to try?
   - What could this solution get you?

8. Give Affirmation: *How is this person taking responsibility for their choices right now?*

9. What would you have to do to get what you want?
   - How would you have to act for that to happen?

10. What conversations would you need to have to get what you want?
    - What kind of person do you need to be to have those conversations?

Build a Plan

- *Which of the possible solutions gets you closest to what you want?*
- *Which one do you think you should pursue?*

1. If you did this, how would it impact your stakeholders?
   - How do you use this information to create your plan?

2. What's the best time and way to go about implementing this plan?

3. How will this decision affect you as a person?

4. Who's someone new that you could bring to the project to enhance it?

5. What steps do you need to consider to ensure that this decision fits with your values?

6. How can this process be fun?

7. How might this solution cause ripples?
   - How does that affect your plan?

8. What support do you need as you resolve this?
   - How do you go about getting that?

9. How are you going to get other people on board with your plan?

10. Give Affirmation: *How is resolving this issue a big deal for this person?*

Insure Action

1. What are you committed to doing differently in order to meet this goal?

2. What will you do if the conflict continues to escalate?

3. What'll motivate you when the going gets tough?

4. How will you celebrate your success?

5. Give Affirmation: *How is this person being a leader right now?*

6. What's a physical object that you can use to remind yourself of this commitment?

7. What should I do if I don't see you taking action?

8. When you think of your priorities, what needs to shift as you add this to your plate?

9. What will 100% commitment look like to you, to meet this goal?
   • What do you have to do to achieve 100% commitment?

10. What does failure with this project look like to you?
    • How do you make sure that doesn't happen?

Final Question:
   So, what are you going to do by when, and how am I going to know?

Give Affirmation (*Answered by the Coach: Choose One*)

1. How do you see this person growing?

2. If you were writing an advertising jingle for this person right now, what would it say?

3. What do you see them doing that is a big deal?

4. Who is this person being right now, and how is that different than a month ago?

5. How is this person in alignment with what's important to them?

■ CLARIFYING GOALS ■

Wonder about Root Cause

1. Where do you need more clarity?

2. How does this situation impact you?

3. What are the areas of conflict/confusion?

4. Bottom line: What's the biggest hurdle you're facing in this situation?

5. Give Affirmation: *What should this person be proud of right now?*

6. What's holding you back from being clear about the situation?

7. What's underneath this confusion? And underneath that?

8. What's your contribution to the problem?

9. What are the potential effects of not clarifying the situation?

10. What frustrates you most about yourself in this situation?
    • What's that about?

Investigate Wants

1. What's your #1 goal in life?
   • What things that we've been discussing will support your #1 goal?

2. What would real success look like in this situation?
   • What does that tell you about the goal?

3. When you are 100 years old, what do you want people to say about you?
   • How does that affect how you want to resolve this situation?

4. Give Affirmation: *How is this person developing new ways of thinking right now?*

5. What is your take on your current goals?
   - What do you want more of and less of with these goals?

6. What would more clarity give you?
   - How do you want to act as you head toward your clarity?

7. In what ways might you hold yourself back as you set this goal?

8. What kind of mark do you want to leave on this earth?
   - How does that impact what you want the goal to look like?

9. What would be the stretch you really want to make here?
   - How does that affect the goal?

10. What is your vision for yourself in the next five years?
    - How does that affect how you want to resolve this situation?

Name Possible Solutions

1. Give Affirmation: *What is outstanding about this person right now?*

2. What's the hardest way to solve this problem?
   - What's the easiest way to gain clarity?

3. What does your gut tell you to do?

4. In the book of *My Perfect Life,* how would this play out?

5. What would a wise grandmother/father tell you to do here?

6. What would you do here, if your life depended on it?

7. How does your decision fit with what's important to you?

8. What would your favorite athlete do in this situation?

9. What would make this situation even more unclear?
   - What's the opposite of that?

10. What would you have to do to gain clarity?
    - How would you have to act for that to happen?

Build a Plan

- *Which of the possible solutions gets you closest to what you want?*
- *Which one do you think you should pursue?*

1. What information do you need to successfully execute the solution?

2. How will this decision affect you as a person?

3. How will you ensure that this decision fits into your big picture?

4. What's a manageable timeline to accomplish this?
   - What would be a stretch timeline?

5. What's the biggest obstacle to your decision?
   - What safeguards do you want to build in to ensure success?

6. Give Affirmation: *How is this person motivating others?*

7. What support do you need to make this a success?
   - How could you ensure that you get that support?

8. What do you need to include to ensure that you're happy about this decision in twelve months?

9. What's the evaluation mechanism for this plan?

10. What's the scariest part of executing this plan?

Insure Action

1. How are you going to let me know that you're moving forward?

2. What happens if it doesn't work out the way you planned?

3. What's the most likely way you'll sabotage your success?
   - How do you want me to be with you if I see that happening?

4. Give Affirmation: *What do you admire about this person right now?*

5. What would stop you from approaching me if you get stuck?
   - What do you need from me to make it easier to approach me?

6. If you can't put a sticky note on your forehead, what else could you do to remember to keep your commitment?

7. How do you want me to help you move forward?

8. What would you have to *stop* doing to successfully execute this plan?

9. What's the most important thing you need to remember as you move forward?

10. What's important about honoring this commitment?

Final Question:

   So, what are you going to do by when, and how am I going to know?

Give Affirmation *(Answered by the Coach: Choose One)*

1. What skills does this person have that will get them where they want to go?

2. What new disciplines is this person successfully learning?

3. What attitudes is this person successfully adopting?

4. Pick an animal you respect. How is this person being like that animal?

5. What three things is this person doing right now that will lead them to success?

■ (LACK OF) AVAILABLE RESOURCES ■

Wonder about Root Cause

1. What might be your blind spot in this situation?
   - If they say, "I don't know," then a good reply would be, "Make it up."

2. How is this like another situation you've experienced?
   - What did you learn from that situation?
   - How can you apply those lessons to this situation?

3. Bottom line: What's the biggest hurdle you're facing in this situation?

4. What is it that you are really missing, that's keeping you from success?

5. Whom/what are you blaming right now for this situation?
   - What's that about?
   - What part is true and what part might not be true?

6. How are you in your own way of success in this situation?

7. Everything is about choice. What choices are you making that contribute to the lack of resources (not necessarily "bad" ones —for example, excellent quality could be one)?

8. Who is one of your heroes?
   - What would that hero be doing differently in this situation?

9. Give Affirmation: *What's one positive thing that you know to be true about this person right now?*

10. What frustrates you most about the fact that this situation exists?

Investigate Wants

1. If you were a songwriter, how would you write the ending?

2. How would you like people to describe you as you resolve this issue?

3. If you could do anything you wanted to reach your goal in this situation, what would you do?

4. If you had total abundance, how would the situation look?

5. What new ways of thinking do you have the opportunity to develop in all of this?

6. If you got what you wanted in this situation, what would you have?

7. Give Affirmation: *What should this person give themselves credit for?*

8. If the word "lack" was not in your vocabulary, what would be different?

9. What do you need to do, to be proud of yourself as you move forward?

10. What's important for you as a person as you move toward resolution?

Name Possible Solutions

1. How would a child solve this problem?
   * How do you want to deal with it?

2. How could you get 100% of what you wanted, 100% of the time in this situation?

3. How would Snow White [insert any character] tackle this issue?

4. What conversations would you need to have to get the resources you desire? With whom do you need to have these conversations?

5. Where haven't you looked for a solution yet?

6. If you had a clean slate and could start from scratch, what would you do to find more resources?

7. Give Affirmation: *How is this person making a difference right now?*

8. What does your gut tell you to do?

9. Everything is about choice. What choices could you make differently to fix the problem? [Be sure to focus on choices like "timeline," "cost," and "quality."]

10. Do you know anyone who has already *un*successfully solved this?
    * What can you learn from them?

Build a Plan
* *Which of the possible solutions gets you closest to what you want?*
* *Which one do you think you should pursue?*

1. What information do you need to create 100% success?

2. How are you going to get what you really want here?

3. What's a new idea that you could bring to the table that would enhance the project?

4. What support or direction do you need to make this a success?
   - How will you get it?

5. How are you going to get other people on board with your plan?

6. What's the one thing that you always forget to build into a plan that you want to build into this one?

7. Give Affirmation: *What type of progress is this person making, and how is that different than a month ago?*

8. What's your backup plan?
   - How will you know when you need to use it?

9. What's the biggest hurdle you'll need to overcome for success?

10. How might this solution change in a month?
    - How will that impact your plan?

Insure Action

1. What happens if the plan fails?

2. What do you need from your colleagues to be successful?

3. Give Affirmation: *How is this person moving toward achieving their goals?*

4. What do you have to take off your plate before you add this to your plate?

5. What would you have to start doing immediately to successfully execute this plan?

6. What's the most important thing you need to remember as you move forward?

7. How can this be a fun and easy process?

8. What'll motivate you when the going gets tough?

9. What should I do if I don't see you doing what you said you would do?

10. What's in it for you if you succeed at this?
    - How will you remind yourself of this?

Final Question:
So, what are you going to do by when, and how am I going to know?

Give Affirmation (*Answered by the Coach: Choose One*)

1. What skills does this person have that will get them where they want to go?

2. What are they doing now that lets you know they'll succeed?

3. What do you see them tackling in a new way?

4. How is this person being a leader right now?

5. How is this person successfully implementing strategies and tactics?

■ DEVELOPMENTAL OPPORTUNITIES ■

Wonder about Root Cause

1. What's going on that has you frustrated?

2. What do you think is *really* causing this situation?

3. In what ways are you not being the person you'd like to be in this situation?

4. What are the areas in which you want to grow/learn?
   - What's going on right now that's in the way of that happening?

5. Which of your buttons are really getting pushed right now?

6. What do you value that's not being respected in this situation?

7. Give Affirmation: *How is this person being true to themselves right now?*

8. What needs to be said here that's not being said?
   - To whom?

9. What's your "dream" career?
   - What appeals to you about that "dream career"?
   - How close does that match your current situation?

10. How are you stopping yourself from growing professionally?

Investigate Wants

1. Name five of your own qualities that you value most.
   - Name three other qualities that you'd like to develop.

2. What is your vision for yourself in the next two years?
   - How does that affect how you want to develop your skills/qualities?

3. What does growth look like to you?

4. Give Affirmation: *What positive qualities is the person showing right now?*

5. If you were going to have four more careers after this one, what would they be?
   - How do those future careers affect your possible solution?

6. Where do you want to go?
   - What kind of person do you want to be as you get there?

7. How do you want to be viewed as you move forward?

8. Where do you want to be moving in your career/life?
   - What qualities and skills do you need to develop as you move in that direction?

9. What kind of animal do you want to be like when resolving this issue?
   - Say more about that.
   - How would you incorporate those traits as you develop your career?

10. What kind of mark do you want to leave on this earth?
    - How does that affect the ways in which you want to develop and grow?

Name Possible Solutions

1. How do you suppose you could improve the situation?

2. If you had 100 choices, how would you choose the right one for you?
   - What's a solution that meets those criteria?

3. What kind of person do you have to "be" to develop in this direction?
   - What do you have to do to get there?

4. What's the solution you've been too afraid to try, or put off trying?
   - What would that solution get you?

5. There are sixteen solutions to any problem: What are four that would move you in the direction you've indicated?

6. Give Affirmation: *How is this person succeeding right now?*

7. If you were a tree in a drought, what would you do to continue to grow in the way you want?

8. Where could you look, or who could you look to, to help you develop the way you want?

9. If you had a clean slate and could start from scratch, what would you do?
   • What in that answer is still possible if you *really* wanted it?

10. What conversations would you need to have to get you what you want?
    • With whom do you need to have these conversations?

Build a Plan
• *Which of the possible solutions gets you closest to what you want?*
• *Which one do you think you should pursue?*

1. How will moving forward in this decision change you as a person?

2. What support do you need to make this a success?

3. Development takes time. How are you going to reprioritize your responsibilities to make this happen?

4. Give Affirmation: *How is this person being heroic right now?*

5. What's the biggest hurdle you'll need to overcome for success?

6. What's the timeline you need to succeed and to stay motivated as you grow?

7. What are you going to do to make this happen?
   • What's the most important part of the plan to execute?

8. How do you ensure that this decision fits into your big-picture career/life goals?

9. What else do you need to take into consideration?
   - Do you need to take anyone else into consideration?

10. How might this solution ruffle some feathers?
    - How will that affect your plan of development?

Insure Action

1. How will you remind yourself to keep moving forward on your development plan?

2. What do you have to say no to, so you can grow and develop?

3. Who else could you talk to who will hold you accountable?

4. What's in it for you if you succeed at this?
   - How will you remind yourself of this?

5. What's the most important thing you need to remember as you move forward?

6. What could possibly trip you up in moving forward?
   - How will you ensure that doesn't happen?

7. What's the best way *for me* to motivate you?

8. Give Affirmation: *How is this person overcoming barriers right now?*

9. What's the impact of not doing this?
   - How are you going to remember that as you move forward?

10. At what stage of a project/plan do you normally lose motivation?
    - What will you do differently for the development goals you've set?

Final Question:
So, what are you going to do by when, and how am I going to know?

Give Affirmation (*Answered by the Coach: Choose One*)

1. How do you see this person growing?

2. In what ways are you excited for this person?

3. What skills does this person have that will get them where they want to go?

4. If you were writing an advertising jingle for this person right now, what would it say?

5. What do you see them doing that is of great importance?

■ LIFE BALANCE ■

Wonder about Root Cause

1. If everything we're talking about is the dying leaf, what's causing the problem at the root of the tree?

2. Give Affirmation: *How/what has this person improved in the past month?*

3. How does being out of balance affect you?

4. So what's *really* causing this imbalance?

5. In what ways are you causing your own imbalance?

6. What's holding you back from staying on an even keel?

7. What's your contribution to the problem?

8. What appeals to you about being off balance?
   - What's that about?

9. What needs to be said here that's not being said?

10. What would your worst enemy say makes you stay out of balance?
    - What would they say is going on?
    - What's true about that?

Investigate Wants

1. What would it take for you to feel balanced?

2. Which of the things that you value is suffering most from being out of balance?
   - What do you value that you're not willing to compromise as you resolve this?

3. What would perfect balance look like?
   - What part of that appeals to you?

4. What type of music do you want to be like when finding your balance?
   - How would you incorporate those traits when resolving this?

5. How would an injured Olympic gymnast find balance on a balance beam?
   - What do you like and dislike about that?

6. How would this have to play out for you to feel good about it?
   - How would you have to act?

7. What does balance look like to you?
   - How does that differ from where you are now?

8. How will the resolution align with who you are as a person?

9. What food dish do you want to be like when resolving this issue?
   - Say more about that.
   - How would you incorporate those traits when resolving this?

10. Give Affirmation: *How is this person moving forward right now?*

Name Possible Solutions

1. What conversations would you need to have to bring you the balance you've described?
   - What would those conversations be like?

2. There are sixteen solutions to any problem: What are four that would move you toward the balance you want?

3. What's the solution that will bring you peace and harmony?

4. What could you do to bring everything back into balance?

5. Who is one of your heroes? What would they do about this issue of balance?

6. What do you have to say no to in order to move toward balance?

7. Give Affirmation: *How does this person remind you of a great leader right now?*

8. What would make you completely out of balance?
   - What's the opposite of that?

9. What do you have to do to get what you *really* want?

10. Name someone with a good life-balance.
    - What do they do that you could apply?

Build a Plan

- *Which of the possible solutions gets you closest to what you want?*
- *Which one do you think you should pursue?*

1. What are you going to do, and when are you going to do it?

2. If you did this, how would it impact the stakeholders/others in your life?
   - How can you use this information to create your plan?

3. How will this decision affect you as a person?

4. What's the biggest obstacle to obtaining the balance you've described?
   • What safeguards do you want to build in to ensure success?

5. Give Affirmation: *How is this person living their values right now?*

6. What's your backup plan if imbalance returns?

7. How will you communicate this plan to others?

8. How do you make this plan as easy and light as possible?

9. With which person do you need to work to succeed at achieving balance?

10. How will you know that this solution is a success?
    • So what do you need to do to get to that definition of success?

Insure Action

1. What are you committed to accomplishing as you move toward balance?

2. Give Affirmation: *In what ways is this person inspiring?*

3. How can I best help you?

4. What's the most likely way you'll sabotage your success at balance?
   • What do you want me to do when I see that happening?

5. How will you celebrate your success?

6. If you can't set a reminder on your computer, what other things could you do to remember to keep your commitment?

7. How often are we going to check in together?

8. What would you have to *stop* doing to successfully execute this plan?

9. What's important about gaining balance?
   - How do you guarantee to remember that moving forward?

10. What does failure look like for you with this plan?
    - How do you make sure that doesn't happen?

Final Question:
   So, what are you going to do by when, and how am I going to know?

Give Affirmation (*Answered by the Coach: Choose One*)

1. How is this person moving outside of their comfort zone?

2. What risks is this person taking, in order to grow and develop?

3. How is this person taking steps to achieve their goals?

4. What struggles do you see this person overcoming?

5. How is this person making a difference in the world?

■ CONFLICTING PRIORITIES ■

Wonder about Root Cause

1. How are you in conflict with yourself?

2. What do you think is *really* causing these priorities to conflict?

3. What's important to you as a person that you're not honoring in this situation?

4. What number are *you* on your list of priorities?
   - What's that about?

5. What needs to be said here that's not being said?
   - To whom?

6. How would your worst enemy describe this situation?
   - What would they say is going on?
   - What's true about that?

7. How does this situation affect you?

8. What are the things/areas that are really in conflict?

9. What frustrates you most about the fact that this conflict of priorities exists?
   - What's important about that?

10. Give Affirmation: *How is this person being willing to go the extra mile right now?*

Investigate Wants

1. What would it look like if nothing conflicted?
   - What appeals to you about that?

2. How would you like the end-state to look so that all the priorities worked out?

3. How would you like the resolution to align with your big-picture priorities?

4. If your priorities were aligned without conflict, what would you have?

5. What do you value that you're not willing to compromise as you resolve this?

6. How could you use this situation to help you move in the direction of your goals?

7. If you chose one priority to the detriment of another, what would it be?
   - How about if you flipped them?
   - What does/doesn't work for you in those scenarios?

8. Give Affirmation: *What is this person shining a light on for others to see?*

9. What would it look like if all the priorities won out?

10. Who is one of your heroes? What would they do about conflicting priorities?
    - How could that apply in your situation?

Name Possible Solutions

1. What would Monty Python [insert any character] do to get you where you want to go?

2. What do you have to do to get a win-win?

3. How would Wile E. Coyote and/or the Road Runner handle this conflict of priorities?

4. If this was a movie, what's the twist no one saw coming?

5. If you only had one priority at work, what would it be?
   - How does that answer impact a solution here?

6. If you had a white board and could start from scratch, how would you design your priorities?

7. What's the tough call you have to make about these priorities that you're avoiding?
   - What do you have to do to move in that direction?

8. Give Affirmation: *How is this person moving toward their goals right now?*

9. What would you have to do to get what you want?
   • How would you have to act for that to happen?

10. What conversation haven't you had that you know would help resolve this conflict?
   • With whom do you need to have these conversations?

Build a Plan

• *Which of the possible solutions gets you closest to what you want?*
• *Which one do you think you should pursue?*

1. If you did this, how will it affect your different priorities?
   • How do you use this information to create your plan?

2. Give Affirmation: *What positive quality do you see in this person that they may not be able to see themselves?*

3. What's a new way of setting priorities that you could use with this plan?

4. How will you know that this solution is a success?
   • So what do you need to do to get to that definition of success?

5. What's the feedback mechanism for this plan?

6. How will you communicate this plan to your colleagues?

7. What do you have to do to bring this to reality?
   • What's the most important part of the plan to execute?

8. How do you ensure that this decision fits into your/the big picture?

9. What advice would your most respected colleague give you right now about building a plan?

10. What's the biggest obstacle to your decision?
    • What safeguards do you want to build in to ensure you overcome this obstacle?

Insure Action

1. How can I help you to be successful here?

2. What do you have to say no to in order to make this happen?

3. Name three other people you could go to, who will hold you accountable.
    • Which of them *will* you talk to?

4. Give Affirmation: *How is this person thinking outside the box right now?*

5. What resources or support do you need to make this happen?
    • How do you go about getting those things?

6. What will you do if people disagree with your plan?

7. How will you celebrate each milestone along the way?

8. How will you become a champion for this cause?

9. What would stop you from approaching me if you get stuck?
    • What do you need from me to make it easier to approach me, if needed?

10. What's in it for you if you succeed at this?
    • How will you remind yourself of this?

Final Question:
   So, what are you going to do by when, and how am I going to know?

Give Affirmation (*Answered by the Coach: Choose One*)

1. How is this person in alignment with what's important to them?

2. What initiatives is this person taking on?

3. What makes this person stand out from the crowd?

4. What hurdles has this person successfully overcome?

5. If you were creating a banner for this person right now, what would it say?

■ DELEGATION ■

Wonder about Root Cause

1. Where are you feeling stuck when it comes to delegating?

2. What's the effect of not delegating effectively?

3. Bottom line: What's the biggest hurdle you're facing when delegating?

4. What's holding you back from delegating more?

5. What are you afraid to delegate?
   • What's that about?

6. Give Affirmation: *How is this person changing for the better?*

7. What might be your blind spot about delegation?
   • [If they say, "I don't know," then a good reply would be, "Make it up."]

8. What's your contribution to not being able to delegate?

9. How would your worst enemy describe this situation?
   • What would they say is going on?
   • What's true about that?

10. What frustrates you most about yourself in this situation?
    - What's that about?

Investigate Wants

1. What would your plate look like if things were perfectly delegated?
   - What appeals and doesn't appeal to you about that?

2. If you were a book author, how would you write the ending to the solution?

3. Give Affirmation: *If this person were to win an award right now, what would it be?*

4. What do you want for your employee as you delegate to them?
   - How do you want to act/be as you delegate to them?

5. What kind of mark do you want to leave on this earth?
   - What would the desired outcome look like in that light?

6. How would you like people to describe you as you resolve this?

7. What is it about delegating that would make you the kind of person you'd like to be?

8. Who is one of your heroes? What would they do about delegating?
   - What do you want to adopt from this hero in this regard?

9. What's your take on delegation?
   - Is there anything about that "take" you'd like to shift?

10. What is your vision for yourself in the next three years?
    - How does that change how you want to resolve this situation?

Name Possible Solutions

1. What could you do to move in the direction you've indicated?

2. How would your favorite athlete or star delegate?

3. How would a woodpecker solve this problem? A lion? A monkey?
   - What appeals to you about these options?

4. Do you know someone who is excellent at delegation?
   - What do they do that you could apply?

5. What's the lose-lose solution?
   - What's the opposite?

6. What do you have to do to stay out of your own way as you delegate?

7. What kind of person do you have to "be" to delegate more?
   - What do you have to do to get there?

8. Give Affirmation: *Where do you see this person going, if they stay moving in the current direction?*

9. What does your gut tell you to do?

10. What would the employees you manage tell you to do?

Build a Plan

- *Which of the possible solutions gets you closest to what you want?*
- *Which one do you think you should pursue?*

1. What are you going to do about this?

2. How do you ensure that this decision fits into who you are as a person?

3. What's the one thing that you always forget to build into a delegation plan that you want to build into this one?

4. What concerns you most about your decision?
   - How do you address this in the plan so it doesn't get in the way?

5. How are you going to get other people on board with your plan?

6. What's your backup plan?
   - How will you know when to use it?

7. What's the biggest hurdle you'll need to overcome for success?
   - How do you address that?

8. What steps do you have to take to get where you want to go?

9. Give Affirmation: *Where do you see this person growing the most right now?*

10. What's the #1 criteria for success?
    - In what ways does that affect your plan?

Insure Action

1. How can I stay out of your way?

2. Give Affirmation: *What new skills do you see this person adopting right now?*

3. What will be the result if you don't follow through on your commitment?
   - How do you remind yourself of that throughout the process?

4. What will have to change in order to pull this off?

5. How can you make this fun?

6. What resources or support do you need to make this happen?
   - How do you go about getting that?

7. What's in it for you if you succeed at this?
   - How will you remind yourself of this?

8. What'll motivate you when the going gets tough?

9. What's a physical object that you can use to remind yourself of this commitment?

10. What does failure with this project look like for you?
    - How can I support you if I see that starting to happen?

Final Question:

So, what are you going to do by when, and how am I going to know?

Give Affirmation (*Answered by the Coach: Choose One*)

1. What do you admire about this person in this situation?

2. How do you see them working in a new way?

3. What new disciplines is this person successfully learning?

4. Who is this person being right now, and how is that different than a month ago?

5. What about this person tells you they'll succeed?

■ INCREASING CONFIDENCE ■

Wonder about Root Cause

1. What are you most afraid of/concerned about in this situation?

2. What's underneath this issue that keeps you from stepping up?

3. What's stopping you in this situation?

4. Give Affirmation: *How is this person being inspiring right now?*

5. On a scale of one to ten, how confident are you in this?
   • What's that about?

6. How is this situation misaligned with who you want to be as a person?

7. Name five qualities of a confident person.
   • How do or don't these show up for you in this situation?

8. What frustrates you most about yourself in this situation?
   • What's that about?

9. What would your best friend say is going on in this situation?
   • That's one way of looking at this situation. Name three other people. What would each of them say is going on in this situation?

10. How is this like another situation you've experienced?
    • What did you learn from that situation?
    • How can you apply those lessons to this situation?

Investigate Wants

1. What would it take for you to feel really confident in this situation?

2. What attitudes do you have the opportunity to develop in all of this?

3. Give Affirmation: *How do you see this person stepping up to the plate right now?*

4. What's the effect of not stepping up here?
   • How is that misaligned with the person you want to be?

5. What would a "confident me" look like?
   • What qualities of that "confident me" do you already have?
   • What qualities of that "confident me" do you want more of?

6. How do you really want to show up, or act, in this situation?

7. What's important for you as a person as you move toward resolution?

8. What is your vision for yourself in the next year?
   - How does that affect how you want to resolve this situation?

9. When you are seventy-five years old, what do you want people to say about you?
   - How does that affect how you want to resolve this situation?

10. How would this have to play out for you to feel more confident?
    - How would you have to act?

Name Possible Solutions

1. How would The Incredibles [insert any character] tackle a lack of confidence?

2. What does your instinct tell you to do?

3. What haven't you tried that you know you need to?

4. How do you really want to show up, or act, in this situation?
   - What do you have to do to get there?

5. What would you do here, if your life depended on it?
   - How does your decision fit with what's important to you?

6. Give Affirmation: *How is this person creating a new behavior right now?*

7. What are the steps you could take to build your confidence in the way you want?

8. What's a solution that would jazz you the most?

9. What do you have to do to continue believing in yourself as you move forward?

10. What would you have to do to get what you want?
    - How would you have to act for that to happen?

Build a Plan

- *Which of the possible solutions gets you closest to what you want?*
- *Which one do you think you should pursue?*

1. What are you going to do to move in the direction you've decided?

2. How will this decision affect you as a person?

3. What feedback will you need to gain the confidence?
   - How will you go about getting that?

4. What are the specific actions you can take to get what you say you want?

5. How do you stay out of your own way as you increase your confidence?

6. What's the biggest obstacle to moving in this direction?
   - How are you going to address that?

7. What do you need to include to ensure that you're happy about this decision in five years?

8. Give Affirmation: *What do you admire in this person right now?*

9. What are three steps you could take today to move in this direction?

10. What support do you need to make this a success?
    - Who can give you that support?
    - When will you talk to them about this?

Insure Action

1. What are you committed to doing differently?
   - How can I help you keep those commitments?

2. How will you keep going when you want to stop?

3. What do you have to say no to in order to make this happen?

4. Is there anyone else you could talk to who will hold you accountable?
   - When will you speak with them?

5. If you can't make a note to yourself, what else could you do to remember to keep your commitment?

6. Give Affirmation: *How is this person being a positive influence right now?*

7. What's the most important thing you need to remember as you start this plan of action?
   - How will you remind yourself of that?

8. What's important to you about this commitment?

9. How will you celebrate this when you start to succeed?

10. What's the best way for me to motivate you if I see you not holding to what you said you wanted to do?

Final Question:
So, what are you going to do by when, and how am I going to know?

Give Affirmation (*Answered by the Coach: Choose One*)

1. What strengths do you see in this person right now?

2. How do you see this person growing?

3. In what ways should this person be proud of themselves?

4. How is this person moving outside of their comfort zone?

5. What risks is this person taking in order to grow and develop?

7

W.I.N. B.I.G. Questions for Any Coaching Situation

If you haven't already done so, you may want to take a look at Chapter 5, "How Do I Use This Book?"

This chapter is divided into six sections, one for each stage of the W.I.N. B.I.G. coaching model. There are forty questions in each section (some have follow-up questions). Remember, your goal is not to ask all of the questions! Have your coachee pick a number between one and forty and use that question to start the dialogue in that section. Follow up with questions of your own, or pick another number. Answer enough questions until you get all of the information you need in that section and then move on.

Reminder: There are italicized "Give Affirmation" questions in each of the sections. If you or your coachee picks one, it is up to the coach (that's you!) to answer it in order to validate the coachee's efforts.

Once you have determined whether the situation at hand is a coachable one, go to the first section, "Wonder about Root Cause— Discovery."

WONDER ABOUT ROOT CAUSE—DISCOVERY

In the first step of coaching, "Wonder about Root Cause," your job is to ask questions that will encourage your employee to curiously examine underlying causes for the issue presented.

1. What is it about this situation that "makes you lose sleep"?

2. If this situation were an onion, what's the problem one layer under this layer?

3. In what ways are you the biggest obstacle here?

4. What might be your blind spot in this situation?
    * [If they say, "I don't know," a good reply would be, "Make it up."]

5. What's confusing you about this situation?

6. Who is one of your heroes? How would that hero describe what's going on in this situation?

7. What do you think is *really* causing this situation?

8. If everything we're talking about is the dying leaf, what's causing the problem at the root of the tree?

9. What frustrates you most about yourself in this situation?
    * What's that about?

10. What seems to be the real trouble?

> Remember to keep this light and fun—coaching does not have to be a long and laborious process!

11. How does this situation affect you?

12. How is this situation misaligned with who you want to be as a person?

13. How is this like another situation you've experienced?
    * What did you learn from that situation?
    * How can you apply those lessons to this situation?

14. Bottom line: What's the biggest hurdle you're facing in this situation?

15. In the bigger scheme of things, how is this important to you?

16. Give Affirmation: *How do you see this person moving outside of their comfort zone in this situation?*

17. In what ways are you not being the person you'd like to be in this situation?

18. What's holding you back from resolving this situation?
    * What's underneath that?

19. How does this situation look to you?

20. What's your contribution to the problem?

> Remember to take the time to check your understanding during this section: "What I hear you saying is that . . ."

21. What keeps you (or has kept you) from having this situation play out the way you'd like?

22. How would an outsider look at this situation?

23. What's the main obstacle here?

24. Which of your buttons are really getting pushed in this situation?

25. What do you value that's not being respected in this situation?

26. What would your best friend say is going on in this situation?
    * That's one way of looking at this situation. Name three other people. What would each of them say is going on in this situation?

27. What are you most afraid of in this situation?

28. What's underneath this issue?

29. What's stopping you in this situation?

30. What does your gut tell you about this situation?

31. What's the real issue?

32. What concerns you most about the situation?

33. How are you "in your own way" in this situation?

34. Who is one of your heroes? What would that hero be doing differently in this situation?
    - What's there to learn from that?

35. Give Affirmation: *In what ways should this person be proud of themselves (as it relates to this situation)?*

36. What frustrates you most about the fact that this situation exists?
    - What's that about?

37. How would your worst enemy describe this situation?
    - What would they say is going on?
    - What's true about that?

38. What's important to you as a person that you're not honoring in this situation?

39. What are the results of not dealing with this situation?

40. What needs to be said in this situation that's not being said?

In this section, continue probing deeper until you get to the root cause. Follow-up questions are important, as are statements that keep the coachee engaged, such as "Tell me more," "Say more about that," and "What else?"

INVESTIGATE WANTS—VISION

In this section, your goal is to help the person clarify what they really want from the situation and *who they want to be as they move in that direction.* Make an effort to remember their answers, because you'll want to refer back to them when you get to problem solving.

You might start off by saying something like:

- It seems like we have a good idea of what's going on, and obviously that's not the way you want it. Let's talk about that for a minute. How do you want this situation to be?
- Wow, so you are up against some pretty big stuff. Let's talk about what it would look like if things were different. Pick a number between one and forty . . .

1. What are the criteria for success here?

2. What does success look like in this situation?

3. What would it take for you to feel really successful in this situation?

4. What qualities will you have to demonstrate to achieve the desired outcome?

5. What is your vision for yourself in the next two years?
   - How does that affect how you want to resolve this situation?

6. How will the resolution align with who you are as a person?

7. Give Affirmation: *What about this person lets you know they'll succeed in this situation?*

8. If you were a screenwriter, how would you write the ending?

9. What do you want in this situation?

10. What do you value that you're not willing to compromise as you resolve this?

11. How would you like people to describe you as you resolve this?

12. If you could do anything you wanted in this situation, what would you do?

13. If you had a magic wand, how would the situation look?

14. What other ideas do you have about what you want?

15. When you are ninety years old, what do you want people to say about you?
    • How does that affect how you want to resolve this situation?

16. How would this have to play out for you to feel good about it?
    • How would you have to act to make that happen?

17. What skills do you have the opportunity to develop in all of this?

18. Give Affirmation: *What do you see in the person that they might not see in themselves that will help them in this situation?*

19. "Paint me a picture" of how you'd like the situation to look.

20. How could you use this to help you move in the direction of your goals?

> If the person answers with an, "I don't know," say, "That's cool, just make it up." The answer may prove to be the right one.

21. What does the desired end-state look like to you?

22. What kind of mark do you want to leave on this earth?
    • How does that affect what you want as you resolve this situation?

23. What does success look like to you in this situation?

24. Take a step away from the issue at hand. How do you want to be as a person?
    • What does the desired outcome look like in that light?

25. What would *real* resolution look like?

26. What household object do you want to be like when resolving this issue?
    • Say more about that.
    • How would you incorporate those traits when resolving this?

27. What are some of your desired outcomes in this situation?

28. Who is one of your heroes? What kind of person would they be in this situation?
    • What do you want to adopt from this hero as you move forward?

29. If you got what you wanted in this situation, what would you have?

30. What kind of person do you want to be as you resolve this situation?

31. What would you like to see happen here?

32. How would someone you disrespect play this out?
    - What do you like and dislike about that option?

33. How will you know when you've succeeded at your solution?

34. What's important for you as a person as you move toward resolution?

35. Give Affirmation: *How is this person making a difference in the world?*

36. How do you want to act as you head toward your desired outcome?

37. If you had no baggage to carry, what would you do in this situation?

38. How do you want to be viewed as you move toward resolution?

39. What do you have to do to be proud of yourself as you move forward?

40. What kind of animal do you want to be like when resolving this issue?
    - Say more about that.
    - How would you incorporate those traits when resolving this?

Again, this is a great place to encourage the coachee to elaborate. Use statements like, "Tell me more," "Say more about that," and "What else?" to expand the conversation.

NAME POSSIBLE SOLUTIONS—PROBLEM SOLVING

The goal of this stage is to help the person become aware of the multitude of possible solutions and choices they have as they move toward their vision. This should have the feel of a brainstorming session. Do not let them get into the nitty-gritty details of action planning (the next section) until you have generated a number of possible solutions.

You might start by saying something like:

- You've got a great idea of who you want to be in this situation. Now let's look at some ideas of how to get there. So based on what you just said that you want. . . .
- It sounds like if all of that happened, you'd be in a great place. Let's talk about the ways you could make it happen. Pick a number between one and forty. Based on what you just said you wanted the situation to look like . . .

1. What are some of the possible solutions here?

2. How would a child solve this problem?

3. How do you suppose you could improve the situation?

4. What would be the riskiest [or pick another: cheapest, most exciting, fastest, etc.] thing you could do?
   - What about that option do you like?

5. What are some other angles to consider?
   - How can we brainstorm more?

Remember to ask all of these questions *based on what they said they wanted* in the "Investigate Wants" section.

6. Let's explore some more—What's the easiest thing to do here?
   - What if you do that? What if you don't?

7. What is another option?

8. How would Indiana Jones [insert any character] tackle this issue?

9. What conversations do you need to have to get you what you want?
   - With whom do you need to have these conversations?

10. There are sixteen solutions to any problem: What are four of them?

11. What's the win-win solution?

12. What could you do to bring everything back into alignment?

13. Who is one of your heroes? What would they do in this situation?

14. What conversation haven't you had that you know would be helpful?

15. Give Affirmation: *What do you see this person tackling in a new way?*

16. What's another choice you could make besides the solutions we've discussed?
    - What might happen if you choose that solution?

17. How would you have solved this problem five years ago?
    - What do you like about that option?

18. If you were eighty-five years old, what would you tell yourself to do?
    - How does the decision affect your big picture?

A great way to check in on possible solutions is to follow up by asking something like, "In what ways does that possibility get you what you want as you move forward?"

19. Where haven't you looked for a solution yet?

20. If you had a clean slate and could start from scratch, what would you do?

21. How could someone else handle this?

22. What would you have to do to get what you want?
    • How would you have to act for that to happen?

23. What have you tried so far that's worth continuing?

24. If this was a movie, what's the twist no one saw coming (as you move to resolution)?

25. Who do you have to "be" to get there? What do you have to do to get there?

26. What's the solution you've been too scared to try?
    • What will this solution get you?

27. Give Affirmation: *What personal traits is this person displaying that lets you know they'll succeed here?*

28. Do you know someone who has already successfully solved a situation like this?
    • What did they do that you could apply?

29. What would you do if you had free reign in this situation?
    • Where would that solution lead?

30. What's the most difficult way to solve this problem?
    • What's the easiest way to have this turn out the way you want?

31. What does your gut tell you to do?

32. What would a wise grandmother/father tell you to do here?

33. What solution would embarrass you the most?
    • What's the opposite of that solution?

34. What haven't you tried that you know would be helpful?

35. What would you do here, if your life depended on it?
    • How does this option fit with what's important to you?

36. What's worked for you in the past in similar situations?

37. How could you get what you want?
    • What would it take to do that?

38. In the book of *My Perfect Life*, how would this play out?

39. What do you have to do to get what you *really* want?

40. What would this look like if it was easy and fun?

Don't move to "Build a Plan" until you have *at least* three to five good possible solutions.

BUILD A PLAN—ACTION

Your goal in this stage is to help the coachee devise a realistic plan that gets them where they want to go in a doable manner and time-frame. Your questions here can get more specific as you help drive the person to a real action plan.

Start this section by asking the first two questions to help the person narrow and choose from the possible solutions they have just developed.

You might start with something like:

- You've got some great possibilities you could pursue. Now let's choose one and look at the details of how to make it happen. [Go to the two lead-in questions.]
- Cool, lots of options, huh? Why don't we narrow them down and talk about how to really make one happen? [Go to the two lead-in questions.]

Always start this section with these questions:

- *Which of the possible solutions gets you closest to what you want?*
- *Which one do you think you should pursue?*

1. What information do you need to execute the solution?

2. What do you need to know about your solution that you don't already know?

3. If you did this, how would it affect your stakeholders?
   - How do you use this information as you create your plan?

4. How will this decision change you as a person?

5. Who's someone new you could bring to the project to enhance your plan?

6. What's the most important part of the plan to execute?

7. How do you ensure that this decision/plan fits into your big picture?

The questions in this section should all pertain to the solution chosen as a result of the first two lead-in questions of this section.

8. What else do you need to take into consideration?

9. What's the biggest obstacle to your plan?
   • What safeguards do you want to build in to ensure success?

10. Give Affirmation: *How have you seen this person successfully implement strategies and tactics that will be helpful in this situation?*

11. What's the one thing you always forget to build into a plan that you want to build into this one?

12. What concerns you most about your decision?

13. What steps do you need to consider to ensure that this decision/plan fits with your values?

14. How can this be fun?

15. What kind of plan do you need to create?

16. How would you pull all this together?

> Remember your ultimate goal here is to drive the person to identify specifics about their action plan.

17. How might this solution cause ripples?
    • How does that affect your plan?

18. What support do you need to make this a success?

19. How are you going to get other people on board with your plan?

20. What resources do you need to ensure success?

21. What do you need to include to ensure that you're happy about this decision in five years?

22. So, what are you going to do to start moving forward?

23. What's the evaluation mechanism for this plan?

24. To what degree will you go to ensure success?

25. What's your backup plan?

26. What's the biggest hurdle you'll need to overcome for success?

27. What's the timeline you need to succeed?

28. What's the first thing you need to do? Then what?

29. With whom do you need to work to succeed?

30. What steps do you have to take to get where you want to go?

31. What do you have to do to get there?
    • What person do you have to "be" to get there?

32. Give Affirmation: *What three qualities do you see in this person that will help them move forward toward success?*

33. What could stop you from moving forward on your decision?
    • What safeguards do you want to build in to ensure success?

34. What's the scariest part of executing this plan?

35. How will you communicate this plan to others?

36. How do you make this plan as easy as possible?

37. What's the feedback mechanism for this plan?

38. When will you get started?

39. What's your game plan (who, what, where, when, why)?

40. How will you know that this solution is a success?
    • So what do you need to do to get there?

Continue to check in on this solution by asking something like, "In what ways does this plan get you what you said you wanted in this situation?"

INSURE ACTION—ACCOUNTABILITY

Your goal here is to help the employee hold true to their commitments by establishing an accountability system.

Be sure to end this section with the given close-out question: So, what are you going to do by when, and how am I going to know?

You might start this section by saying something like:

- OK, you've got a great plan, and I also know you have a lot of other things waiting for you back on your desk. Let's spend a few minutes talking about how we can make sure this doesn't get buried by something else. Pick a number between one and forty . . .

> Your intent here is not to be a nag or a micro-manager. Your intent is to help keep the employee's commitments in the forefront of their mind so that they can be successful. Ask your questions with that intent and with that mindset.

- This all sounds great. I really want to see you do this, so to be sure, I want to help hold you accountable to what you've said you want to achieve. Pick a number between one and forty . . .

1. What part of this plan are you most committed to?

2. How can you make this fun?

3. How are you going to let me know that you're moving forward?

4. What happens if you hit a snag and it doesn't work out the way you planned?

5. What'll motivate you when the going gets tough?

6. How will you remind yourself to do this [work on this] on a regular basis?

7. At what stage of a project do you normally lose motivation?
   - What will you do differently for this plan?

8. What's the best way for you to circle back to me on this?

9. How will you keep going when you want to quit?

10. What do you have to say no to in order to make this happen?

11. Is there anyone else you could talk to who will hold you accountable to your plan?

12. How can I stay out of the way of your success?

13. How will you celebrate your success?

14. What does failure look like for you with this plan?
    - How do you make sure that doesn't happen?

15. What resources do you need to make this happen?
    - What challenges might that present for you?

16. What do you need from me to be successful?

17. What's in it for you if you succeed at this?
    - How will you remind yourself of this?

18. Give Affirmation: *If you were creating a banner for this person right now, what would it say?*

19. What should I do if I don't see you taking action?

Be sure to take notes for yourself. You will be responsible for holding this person accountable, so you will need to follow through on your commitments.

20. When you think of your priorities, what needs to shift as you add this to your plate?

21. What's the result if you don't follow through on your commitment?

22. What's a physical object that you can use to remind yourself of this commitment?

23. How can I best support you during this process?

24. What's the most likely way you'll sabotage your success?
    - How do you want me to be with you when I see that happening?

25. Give Affirmation: *In what ways is this person inspiring?*

26. How do you want me to help you celebrate your progress?

27. What would stop you from approaching me if you get stuck?
    - What do you need from me to make it easier to approach me?

28. What direction do you need from me?

29. If you can't tie a string on your finger, what else could you do to help you remember to keep your commitment?

30. How often are we going to check in together?

31. What do you have to take off your plate before you put this on your plate?

32. What would you have to stop doing to successfully execute this plan?

33. How can I run defense for you?

34. Give Affirmation: *What strengths do you see in this person right now?*

35. If you were going to put a sticky note on your computer to keep you motivated, what would it say?

36. What happens if the project fails?
    - What safeguard can you put in place to ensure success?

37. What's the most important thing you need to remember as you move forward?

38. What's important about honoring this commitment?

39. What's the best way for me to motivate you?

40. What's the result of not doing this?
    - How are you going to remember that as you move forward?

Be sure to end this section with the given close-out question: So, what are you going to do by when, and how am I going to know?

If using this book on your own, answer any of the questions above, in addition to these:

1. Whom can you talk to who will help hold you accountable to your plan?

2. What do you need from that person in order to be successful?

3. What physical object (a sticky note on your computer, a rubber band on your water bottle, etc.) can you use to help remind yourself of your plan?

4. What will you do, by when, and how will you let someone know you've done it?

GIVE AFFIRMATION—VALIDATE

Your purpose in this section is to validate the goals, efforts, and plans that the person is putting forth and to validate the strengths or qualities that you see, think, or know will make them successful as they move forward. [In this section you (the coach) answer the questions.]

You could start by saying something like:

- This is great. You've got a solid plan. I just want to take a second and point out what you've done here . . .
- OK, before we end, I just want to take a second to validate the effort you've made. Pick a number between one and forty . . .

These questions are meant to be starters. You may want to add some of your own as you acknowledge the person for what they've done, who they are, and what they've committed to do. Real validation has to come from *you*, not a book!

Answered by the coach:

1. What strengths do you see in this person right now?

2. What about this person lets you know they'll succeed?

3. What do you admire about this person in this situation?

4. What about this person makes you believe they'll be successful with the plan?

5. In what ways should this person be proud of themselves?

6. In what ways are you excited for this person?

7. If you were creating a banner for this person right now, what would it say?

8. What do you see in the person that they might not see in themselves?

9. What skills does this person have that will get them where they want to go?

10. What is this person already doing that lets you know they'll succeed?

11. What do you see this person tackling in a new way?

12. What are some strengths you think this person should remember about themselves as they move forward?

13. What type of progress has this person made?

14. If you were writing an advertising jingle for this person right now, what would it say?

15. What do you see this person doing that is a big deal?

16. What do you see this person doing that is a step forward?

When answering these questions, use *complete sentences* and be specific. Don't just read the question and answer by saying, for example, "inspiring." Say something like, "I see you being a leader right now because you're inspiring. You are dedicated to getting this done quickly and to finding a way for the whole team to benefit—that's inspiring."

17. How is this person behaving differently now than in the past?

18. What contributions is this person giving to the world?

19. What new habits is this person implementing?

20. What new disciplines is this person successfully learning?

21. What attitudes is this person successfully adopting?

22. How is this person being a leader right now?

23. How is this person successfully implementing strategies and tactics?

24. If you were going to give this person an award right now, what would it be for?

25. What initiatives is this person taking on?

26. How is this person moving outside of their comfort zone?

27. What risks is this person taking in order to grow and develop?

28. How is this person taking steps to achieve their goals?

29. In what ways is this person inspiring?

30. What five qualities do you see in this person right now that will help them move forward?

31. Who is this person being right now, and how is that different than a month ago?

32. How is this person in alignment with what's important to them?

33. If you were toasting this person at a party, what is the most important thing you would say about them?

34. What makes this person stand out from the crowd?

35. How is this person motivating others?

36. Pick an animal you respect. How is this person being like that animal?

37. What struggles are you witnessing this person work through?

38. What hurdles are you witnessing this person successfully overcome?

39. What three things is this person doing right now that will lead them to success?

40. How is this person making a difference in the world?

If you are using this book on your own, answer at least two of the following questions:

1. How is all of this helping you move toward becoming the person that you want to be?

2. What are three things in all of this that you should give yourself credit for?

3. Pick an animal you respect. How are you being like that animal right now?

4. In what ways are you proud of yourself for working through this issue?

5. What's one positive thing that you know is true about yourself right now?

6. What qualities would your best friend say you are exhibiting right now?

7. In what ways would you stand out from a crowd right now?

8. Who is one of your heroes? In what ways are you being like them right now?

9. In what ways are you being "the person you want to be" right now?

10. What's something that you are doing/plan on doing in all of this that is a stretch for you?
    - How does that stretch excite you?

11. You can also answer as many of the questions as you'd like from the forty above by replacing "this person" with "you." Go ahead, you deserve it.

Index

About the Authors

After graduating from Cornell University's Hotel School, **Anne Loehr** managed successful hotels and "green" businesses in Europe, Africa, and the United States for over 15 years. Her "green" work has been featured in *Newsweek International, National Geographic Traveler, Elle Canada, Outside Magazine, CNN Money, Sunday Times* (UK), *Guardian* (UK), and other international press. In an effort to find top-quality leadership, coaching, and team effectiveness facilitators for her 500 Kenyan employees, she started studying these skills herself and became a certified coach. Anne has since partnered with leaders at The Away Network, World Bank, Campbell's, The Nature Conservancy, and Carlson Destination Marketing Services.

Brian Emerson, a certified coach, created Riverstone Endeavors, an organizational-development firm that partners with leaders as they determine how to get the best out of their employees and organizations (www.riverstoneendeavors .com). His expertise includes team effectiveness, leadership development, and strategic/cultural alignment. He collaborates with organizations to develop lasting solutions to the "chronic un-solvable problems" that stand in the way of high performance. Brian has partnered with clients such as PBS, Natural Resources Defense Council, Airlines Reporting Corporation (ARC), Howard Hughes Medical Institute, and MedImmune.

Both based in the Washington, DC, area, Anne and Brian have worked together for a number of years consulting to organizations, writing articles, and speaking at conferences and workshops. Their love of travel led them to create "Safaris for the Soul" (www.safarisforthesoul.com), leadership-development retreats that use the world as a classroom to help senior managers discover how to be more effective in leading their organizations to success. These trips take place around the world and have been featured in *The Washingtonian, Business Traveler,* and *Body+Soul.*